Narration and Therapeutic Action

The Construction of Meaning in Psychoanalytic Social Work

Narration and Therapeutic Action

The Construction of Meaning in Psychoanalytic Social Work

Jerrold R. Brandell, PhD
Editor

The Haworth Press, Inc.
New York · London

Narration and Therapeutic Action: The Construction of Meaning in Psychoanalytic Social Work has also been published as *Journal of Analytic Social Work*, Volume 3, Numbers 2/3 1996.

The development, preparation, and publication of this work has been undertaken with great care. However, the publisher, employees, editors, and agents of The Haworth Press and all imprints of The Haworth Press, Inc., including The Haworth Medical Press and Pharmaceutical Products Press, are not responsible for any errors contained herein or for consequences that may ensue from use of materials or information contained in this work. Opinions expressed by the author(s) are not necessarily those of The Haworth Press, Inc.

The Haworth Press, Inc., 10 Alice Street, Binghamton, NY 13904-1580 USA

Library of Congress Cataloging-in-Publication Data

Brandell, Jerrold R.
    Narration and therapeutic action : the construction of meaning in psychoanalytic social work / Jerrold R. Brandell.
       p. cm.
    Also published as Journal of analytic social work, v. 3, no. 2/3, 1996.
    Includes bibliographical references and index.
    ISBN 1-56024-827-0 (alk. paper)
      1. Personal construct therapy. 2. Psychoanalysis. 3. Constructivism (Psychology). 4. Psychiatric social work. I. Journal of analytic social work. II. Title.
RC489.P46B7 1996
616.89'14–dc20
                                           96-20074
                                           CIP

INDEXING & ABSTRACTING

Contributions to this publication are selectively indexed or abstracted in print, electronic, online, or CD-ROM version(s) of the reference tools and information services listed below. This list is current as of the copyright date of this publication. See the end of this section for additional notes.

- *Abstracts in Anthropology*, Baywood Publishing Company, 26 Austin Avenue, P. O. Box 337, Amityville, NY 11701

- *Applied Social Sciences Index & Abstracts (ASSIA) (Online: ASSI via Data-Star) (CDRom: ASSIA Plus)*, Bowker-Saur Limited, Maypole House, Maypole Road, East Grinstead, West Sussex RH19 1HH, England

- *caredata CD: the social and community care database*, National Institute for Social Work, 5 Tavistock Place, London WC1H 9SS, England

- *CNPIEC Reference Guide: Chinese National Directory of Foreign Periodicals*, P.O. Box 88, Beijing, Peoples Republic of China

- *Criminal Justice Abstracts*, Willow Tree Press, 15 Washington Street, 4th Floor, Newark, NJ 07102

- *Criminolgy, Penology and Police Science Abstracts*, Kugler Publications, P. O. Box 11188, 1001 GD Amsterdam, The Netherlands

- *Digest of Neurology and Psychiatry*, The Institute of Living, 400 Washington Street, Hartford, CT 06106

- *Family Studies Database (online and CD/ROM)*, Peters Technology Transfer, 306 East Baltimore Pike, 2nd Floor, Media, PA 19063

- *Family Violence & Sexual Assault Bulletin*, Family Violence & Sexual Assault Institute, 1310 Clinic Drive, Tyler, TX 75701

- *IBZ International Bibliography of Periodical Literature*, Zeller Verlag GmbH & Co., P.O.B. 1949, D-49009 Osnabruck, Germany

- *INNOVATIONS AND RESEARCH*, NAMI/Boston University, 730 Commonwealth Avenue, Boston, MA 02215

(continued)

- *International Bulletin of Bibliography on Education*, Proyecto B.I.B.E./Apartado 52, San Lorenzo del Escorial, Madrid, Spain

- *INTERNET ACCESS (& additional networks) Bulletin Board for Libraries ("BUBL"), coverage of information resources in INTERNET, JANET, and other networks.*
  - JANET X.29:UK.AC.BATH.BUBL or 00006012101300
  - TELNET: BUBL.BATH.AC.UK or 138.38.32.45 login 'bubl'
  - Gopher: BUBL.BATH.AC.UK (138.32.32.45). Port 7070
  - World Wide Web: http: //www. bubl.bath.ac.uk./BUBL/ home.html
  - NISSWAIS: telnetniss.ac.uk (for the NISS gateway) The Andersonian Library, Curran Building, 101 St. James Road, Glasgow G4 ONS, Scotland

- *Mental Health Abstracts (online through DIALOG)*, IFI/ Plenum Data Company, 3202 Kirkwood Highway, Wilmington, DE 19808

- *NIAAA Alcohol and Alcohol Problems Science Database (ETOH)*, National Institute on Alcohol Abuse and Alcoholism, 1400 Eye Street NW, Suite 600, Washington, DC 20005

- *Periodica Islamica*, Berita Publishing, 22 Jalan Liku, 59100 Kuala Lumpur, Malaysia

- *Referativnyi Zhurnal (Abstracts Journal of the Institute of Scientific Information of the Republic of Russia)*, The Institute of Scientific Information, Baltijskaja ul., 14, Moscow A-219, Republic of Russia

- *Sage Family Studies Abstracts (SFSA)*, Sage Publications, Inc., 2455 Teller Road, Newbury Park, CA 91320

- *Social Work Abstracts*, National Association of Social Workers, 750 First Street NW, 8th Floor, Washington, DC 20002

(continued)

- ***Sociological Abstracts (SA)***, Sociological Abstracts, Inc., P. O. Box 22206, San Diego, CA 92192-0206

- ***Studies on Women Abstracts***, Carfax Publishing Company, P. O. Box 25, Abingdon, Oxfordshire OX14 3UE, United Kingdom

SPECIAL BIBLIOGRAPHIC NOTES

related to special journal issues (separates)
and indexing/abstracting

☐ indexing/abstracting services in this list will also cover material in any "separate" that is co-published simultaneously with Haworth's special thematic journal issue or DocuSerial. Indexing/abstracting usually covers material at the article/chapter level.

☐ monographic co-editions are intended for either non-subscribers or libraries which intend to purchase a second copy for their circulating collections.

☐ monographic co-editions are reported to all jobbers/wholesalers/approval plans. The source journal is listed as the "series" to assist the prevention of duplicate purchasing in the same manner utilized for books-in-series.

☐ to facilitate user/access services all indexing/abstracting services are encouraged to utilize the co-indexing entry note indicated at the bottom of the first page of each article/chapter/contribution.

☐ this is intended to assist a library user of any reference tool (whether print, electronic, online, or CD-ROM) to locate the monographic version if the library has purchased this version but not a subscription to the source journal.

☐ individual articles/chapters in any Haworth publication are also available through the Haworth Document Delivery Services (HDDS).

Narration and Therapeutic Action
The Construction of Meaning in Psychoanalytic Social Work

CONTENTS

∞   ALL HAWORTH BOOKS AND JOURNALS
    ARE PRINTED ON CERTIFIED
    ACID-FREE PAPER

ABOUT THE EDITOR

Jerrold R. Brandell, PhD, is Associate Professor at the Wayne State University School of Social Work, where he serves as chairperson of the graduate concentration in mental health.

Dr. Brandell received his master's degree in social work from the University of Wisconsin at Madison, and his doctorate from the University of Chicago. He has had advanced training in psychoanalytic psychotherapy, hypnotherapy, and hypnoanalysis, and is currently a candidate in the program in psychoanalysis at the Michigan Psychoanalytic Council. Dr. Brandell held an Edith Abbott Doctoral Teaching Fellowship at the University of Chicago, and taught at both the Michigan State University and Boston University Schools of Social Work prior to his current appointment at Wayne State University. He has also served as a member of the Continuing Education Faculty at the Summer Program at Smith College School of Social Work. Dr. Brandell was the contributing editor of an interdisciplinary volume entitled, *Countertransference in Psychotherapy with Children and Adolescents*, published in 1992 (Jason Aronson, Inc.), and is preparing another volume due to be published in 1997 by The Free Press, tentatively entitled, *Theory and Practice in Clinical Social Work*.

Dr. Brandell has published in the areas of dynamic child psychotherapy and the didactic and supervisory use of therapeutic process analysis. He has presented papers at both national and international conferences in psychoanalysis, clinical social work, psychology, and psychiatry, and recently lectured in Israel at the invitation of the University of Haifa and Bar-Ilan University. He is actively engaged in private clinical practice, consultation, and clinical supervision in the Detroit and Ann Arbor areas.

Introduction

Jerrold R. Brandell

Interest in the study of narratives, and the process by which meaning is "created" through shared discourse has gradually filtered from the humanities and social sciences into the disciplinary domains of both psychoanalysis and clinical social work. The analysis of narrative discourse is found in such disparate fields of inquiry as cultural anthropology, psychology, (Mellard, 1987), philosophy (Ricoeur, 1981), history (White, 1973), ethics (McIntyre, 1984), literature (Booth, 1979), and linguistics. In sociolinguistic terms, *narratives* are organized units of discourse whose essential internal function consists of the recounting of a story (Hoshmand, 1993). Narration enables the narrator to capture past experience or construct present or future experience and as such, involves a temporal sequence (Labov & Waletzky, 1967). Narratives can be described as "natural cognitive and linguistic forms through which individuals attempt to order, organize, and express meaning" (Mishler, 1986, p. 106). Though there may not be complete consensus on how narrative ought be defined, there is fundamental agreement that narratives should organize events so that "a sense of coherence as well as a sense of direction or movement over time" (Borden, 1992, p.136) is clearly demonstrated.

Clinical social work, psychology, and other human sciences appear to be in a transitional period in which basic assumptions about what constitutes science and scientific inquiry are being challenged. The positivistic worldview, which has exerted a powerful and pervasive influence on modern scientific thought, has also imposed significant constraints on the nature of research within the clinical professions (Howard, 1985; Mahoney, 1991; Polkinghorne, 1984, 1991; Neimeyer & Neimeyer, 1993). As theorists have become increasingly aware of such restrictions, efforts to cultivate and distill methods of investigation derived from other disciplines that are

[Haworth indexing entry note]: "Introduction." Brandell, Jerrold R. Published in: *Narration and Therapeutic Action: The Construction of Meaning in Psychoanalytic Social Work* (ed: Jerrold R. Brandell) The Haworth Press, Inc., 1996, pp. 1-7. Single or multiple copies of this article are available from The Haworth Document Delivery Service [1-800-342-9678, 9:00 a.m. - 5:00 p.m. (EST) E-mail address: getinfo@haworth.com].

less bound by the assumptions of positivistic science have increased (Nei-meyer & Neimeyer, 1993). Consequently, clinical scholars have begun to consider such issues or approaches as self-agency, hermeneutics, semeiotics, and theories that emphasize intentional action and narrative knowing (ibid).

> We are seeing in our lifetimes the collapse of the objectivist world-view that dominated the modern era, the worldview that gave people faith in the absolute and permanent rightness of certain beliefs and values. The worldview that is emerging in its place is constructivist. If we operate from this worldview we see all information and all stories as human creations that fit, more or less well, with our experience and within a universe that remains always beyond us and always mysterious. (Anderson, 1990, p. 268)

The common assumption shared by all constructivist orientations has been described in the following manner: No one has "access to a singular, stable, and fully knowable reality. All of our understandings instead" are embedded in social and interpersonal contexts, and are therefore limited in perspective, depth, and scope. Constructivist approaches appear to have a common guiding premise that informs all thinking about the nature of knowing. In effect, constructivist thinking assumes that human beings (1) are naturally and actively engaged in efforts to understand the totality of their experiences in the world, (2) are not able to gain direct access to external realities, and (3) are continually evolving and changing (Neimeyer & Neimeyer, 1993, pp. 2-3). Constructivism and the study of narratives are therefore the study of *meaning-making*. As human beings, we are compelled to interpret experience, to search for purpose, to understand the significance of the events and scenarios in which we play a part.

In this collection, eight contributors examine various aspects of narrative theory and its relationship to psychoanalysis and clinical social work. The contributions are quite varied, and range from the highly abstract and theoretical to those that consider very specific dimensions of clinical process.

The first article, entitled "The Contributions of Roy Schafer and Donald Spence to the Study of Narrative," is written by Patricia Sweetser. This scholarly contribution describes and explicates the meanings given to the term "narrative" in the work of two important psychoanalytic theorists. Sweetser begins with a discussion of Schafer's concept of "action language," a precursor to his later excursions into the study of narrative. Action language, Sweetser asserts, was originally intended as Schafer's challenge to Freudian metapsychology and its undergirding in nineteenth century natural science. As his work evolved, Schafer began to recast psychoanalytic theories as narratives, and ultimately, to consider how narration functions within the psychoanalytic dialogue itself. Schafer, Sweetser observes, came to the study of narrative only gradually, whereas Donald Spence actually began his work with considerations of narration and its relationship to the psychoanalytic process. Spence has argued, particularly in his earlier work, that the reliance on the classical model of *reconstruction*, with its emphasis on historical truth, is inherently flawed inasmuch as it treats narrative truths *as though* they were historical truths. Sweetser describes this position in substantial detail, and follows with further exploration of the points of convergence and divergence in the work of these two seminal thinkers.

In the second paper, "Paradigms, Metaphors, and Narratives: Stories We Tell About Development," Joseph Palombo examines the status of developmental theories, and how such concepts as *paradigm*, *metaphor*, and *narrative* may be applied to psychoanalytic developmental theories. Palombo makes the argument that the use of metaphors is central to the construction of developmental theories, and further contends that metaphors are used as explanatory models in *all* developmental theories. Whether or not a theory has a narrative structure depends upon the type of metaphor used. Palombo examines a range of theories and the metaphors in which they are rooted (e.g., Freud's mechanistic/hydraulic model; Basch's information processing theory; Freud's ingestion model; Mahler's embryological model; and Kohut's translocation model). He is critical of constructivist approaches to theory-making because they cannot adequately establish the relationship between a subject's current difficulty and its historical emergence. He observes that sole reliance on the criterion of coherence in order to create meaning ("knit[ting] together the narrative") is unsatisfactory; 'coherence' used in this way obviates the need for a "bridge" between historical past and present. Palombo concludes by asserting a "psychoanalytic developmental theory consistent with self psychology" as the only theory among many considered that might ultimately attain the status of a *paradigm* ("a set of hypotheses that articulate universal propositions about the course of development").

In their paper, "Deconstruction and Reconstruction: A Self-Psychological Perspective on the Construction of Meaning in Psychoanalysis," Maria Miliora and Richard Ulman make the argument that psychoanalysis is both a science of hermeneutics, concerned with discovering the meaning of the subject's experience through his/her language, *and* a science in the positivist tradition (i.e., concerned with cause and effect). Recent criticisms of psychoanalysis have tended to adhere to either one view or the other, creating what the authors refer to as a "discursive chasm" in the debate over the role of meaning in contemporary conceptualizations of psychoanalysis. The authors propose that psychoanalysis is fundamentally hermeneutic *and* causal, a "hermeneutic science concerned with the . . . interpretation and analysis of the unconscious meaning of experience." They then proceed to discuss the work of Kohut and the concept of the selfobject, claiming that there is a cause-and-effect interrelationship among fantasy, meaning, and symptom that is based upon particular abnormal self/selfobject experiences occurring in early development. The remainder of the paper focuses on clinical studies of patients with panic disorder, obsessive-compulsive disorder, and obsessive-compulsive personality disorder. In two clinical illustrations, Miliora and Ulman demonstrate how both meaning and causality can be incorporated and integrated in a self-psychological view of psychopathology.

"A Sense of Orders: An Introduction to the Theory of Jacques Lacan," written by Barbara Berger, provides a basic introduction to Lacanian ideas and conceptual schemas. Lacan was a French analyst who exerted a profound influence on psychoanalysis in France and elsewhere in Europe, but who has had only modest impact on psychoanalytic thought in this country. Lacan emphasized the relationship of language to the unconscious, claiming that language structures the unconscious. Insofar as the unconscious has a structure that is determined by language, it is revealed in the discourse between analyst and the patient. Berger discusses several central Lacanian ideas, including his "triad of orders" (the Real, the Symbolic, and the Imaginary), and clinical illustrations. She also provides a thoughtful discussion of the Lacanian notions of trauma, fixation, reproduction, and transference. She asserts that a major Lacanian contribution was the idea that meaning is revealed by signification: signifiers (i.e., words), must ultimately be linked to the signifieds, (i.e., "the original, unconscious thoughts which are barred from speech").

In her paper, "Adult Re-Collections of Childhood Sexual Abuse," Janice Gasker questions whether newly-emerging memories of traumas from the remote past have historical accuracy and historical "truth," or are simply "constructions," life stories or narratives that are knit or pieced together but lack veridicality. In her systematic effort to address this question, Gasker examines psychoanalytic drive theory, the concept of dissociation, cognitive psychological theory, and folkloristic studies, *inter alia*. Gasker's emphasis on such notions as *collaborative meaning-making*, *embodied cognition*, and the *social context of the narrative* leads her to question the usefulness of any search for "absolute" truth. She proposes a reality that is interactive and intersubjective, and always context-dependent. Gasker concludes with the proposition that both client and therapist can be empowered as co-authorship of a jointly woven text, or as "co-creators of a life narrative."

In the next paper, "Narrative Re-Telling in Clinical Treatment: A Single Case Study," Catherine H. Nye offers a detailed consideration of the "telling and retelling" of a particular narrative over a two and one half year course of psychoanalysis. In the commentary and analysis that the author provides, significant alterations in the structure and content of the client's account are carefully noted. This allows for a more complete appreciation of the evolution of the narrative process, and furthermore, of the relationship that the narrative has to other aspects of the treatment. Nye makes the point that repeated tellings of a particular narrative are often made in the service of mastering difficult aspects of personal experience of a traumagenic nature. Client references to the narrative in this case are actually made on ten different occasions over a span of 324 sessions. Nye identifies several phases of the narrative process: in the initial telling, the facts of the story are presented without detail or elaboration; in the second phase, affect is explored, there is elaboration of the context surrounding the story, and meaning emerges from the analyst-client discourse; finally, in the third phase the fully elaborated narrative that had earlier emerged (in the second phase) is "distilled to its essential components."

Thomas M. Young, in "Using Narrative Theory and Self Psychology Within a Multigenerational Family Systems Perspective," attempts to integrate narrative concepts and aspects of psychoanalytic self psychology within the overarching perspective of multigenerational family systems theory. In several sections, the author discusses various aspects of both psychoanalytic self psychology and narrative theory, emphasizing their fundamental complementarity. Young then asserts that the content, structure, and meanings of a client's narratives are more fully understood when they are viewed in the context of the multigenerational family system. This perspective allows both client and therapist to apprehend the important relationship between the client's stories and the intercurrent conflicts and issues these stories represent. Whether they are principally intrapsychic or interpersonal stories derived from and are imbedded in the culture and history of the narrator's family of origin. To illustrate how such thinking can enhance and amplify the process of psychoanalytic psychotherapy, Young presents a detailed reconstruction of his clinical work with an adult client who had sought therapy for relief from a long-standing depression.

In the final contribution to this collection, Barbara Socor provides us with a provocative and enlightening discussion of Steiner's work. *Real Presences* is a collection of essays that Socor believes can offer the psychoanalytically oriented clinician "fertile and stimulating ways of approaching the challenges presented to our profession by deconstructive theory." She observes that Steiner's essays are probably most usefully described as "philosophical ponderings on the nature of language and the aesthetic enterprise in the absence of metaphysical meaning."

It may be argued that the clinical focus in both social work and psychoanalysis has become inextricably interwoven with considerations of narrative form and meaning. Such considerations raise important questions about the very nature of what is therapeutic in the psychoanalytic process and why; whether existing theory can be used with modification as a guide to the 'unpacking' of the text; if there are specific psychoanalytic theories of development better-suited to the meaning-making that occurs in the crucible of the psychoanalytic dialogue, and so on. In the pages that follow, many such questions are raised and considered in light of the relationship of narration to the therapeutic action of psychoanalytic social work. The reader will find abundant evidence of both consensus and conflict, disparity and complementarity, resonance and dissonance in the variable points of view represented in these eight contributions. Perhaps it could not be otherwise. But it is equally true that the ultimate value of a collection such as this, like the subject matter of the volume itself, can never be judged apart from each individual reader's construction of meaning. It is in this spirit that these eight papers are offered.

REFERENCES

Anderson, W.T. (1990). *Reality isn't what it used to be.* New York: Harper & Row.

Booth, W. (1979). *Critical understanding.* Chicago: University of Chicago Press.

Borden, W. (1992). Narrative perspectives in psychosocial intervention following adverse life events. *Social Work, 37,* 135-141.

Hoshmand, L. (1993). The personal narrative in the communal construction of self and life issues. in G. Neimeyer (Ed.), *Constructivist assessment: A casebook,* (pp. 179-205). Newbury Park, CA: Sage Publications.

Howard, G. (1985). Can research in the human sciences become more relevant to practice? *Journal of Counseling and Development, 63,* 539-544.

Labov, W., & Waletzky, J. (1967). Narrative analysis. In J. Helm (Ed.), *Essays on the verbal and visual arts,* (pp. 12-44). Seattle: University of Washington Press.

McIntyre, A. (1984). *After virtue.* Notre Dame, IN: Notre Dame University Press.

Mahoney, M.J. (1991). *Human change processes.* New York: Basic Books.

Mishler, E. (1986). *Research interviewing: Context and narrative.* Cambridge, MA: Harvard University Press.

Neimeyer, G. (1993). Defining the boundaries of constructivist assessment. In G.

Neimeyer (Ed.), *Constructivist assessment: A casebook*, (pp. 1-30). Newbury Park, CA: Sage Publications.

Polkinghorne, D.E. (1988). *Narrative knowing and the human sciences*. New York: State University of New York Press.

Ricoeur, P. (1981). *Hermeneutics and the human sciences*. Cambridge, England: Cambridge University Press.

White, H. (1973). *Metahistory: The historical imagination in nineteenth century Europe*. Baltimore: Johns Hopkins University Press.

Chapter 1

The Contributions of Roy Schafer and Donald Spence to the Study of Narrative

Patricia Sweetser

SUMMARY. This review considers the sense given to the term "narrative" in the work of Roy Schafer and Donald Spence. Roy Schafer's interest in narrative came through his concept of action language, which was an attempt to challenge and revise traditional Freudian metapsychology. Emphasis upon narrative has given Schafer a new view upon traditional theory and practice. Although Spence is equally iconoclastic and challenging, his use of the term differs markedly from Schafer's. The study contrasts the different positions Spence and Schafer arrived at through exploration of narrative, particularly their different attitudes to the problem of verifiability. *[Article copies available from The Haworth Document Delivery Service: 1-800-342-9678. E-mail address: getinfo@haworth.com].*

Roy Schafer and Donald Spence both contributed significantly to the work linking narrative and psychoanalytic psychotherapy. Schafer's ideas on narrative developed over a period of years during which he emphasized

Patricia Sweetser, PhD, MSW, is affiliated with Mt. Tom Institute, Holyoke, MA.

[Haworth co-indexing entry note]: "The Contributions of Roy Schafer and Donald Spence to the Study of Narrative." Sweetser, Patricia. Co-published simultaneously in *Journal of Analytic Social Work* (The Haworth Press, Inc.) Vol. 3, No. 2/3, 1996, pp. 9-29; and: *Narration and Therapeutic Action: The Construction of Meaning in Psychoanalytic Social Work* (ed: Jerrold R. Brandell) The Haworth Press, Inc., 1996, pp. 9-29. Single or multiple copies of this article are available from The Haworth Document Delivery Service [1-800-342-9678, 9:00 a.m. - 5:00 p.m. (EST) E-mail address: get info@haworth.com].

their evolution, letting them be seen as in process rather than as fully determined. Spence's major work appeared after much of Schafer's work, and Spence is openly indebted to Schafer for parts of his work, so there is a tradition of sorts here, not a clear line of development perhaps, but a continuity of concerns and themes. Both consider how narrative shapes our hearing within the clinical encounter and view theory as a socially determined construction most usefully understood as a form of narrative. To narrate (L. *gnoscere*) is to know, so the study of narration becomes the study of knowledge; the nature of meaning and perception are brought within the field of study. Schafer and Spence address these broader implications of narrative while still attending to clinical issues.

THE CONTRIBUTIONS OF ROY SCHAFER

A reader wishing to see Schafer's ideas on narrative in their fullest development should consult his latest book, *Retelling a Life: Narration and Dialogue in Psychoanalysis* (1992). There Schafer smoothly, richly, and sometimes elegantly weaves into a coherent whole the themes and concerns of the past twenty years of his work. What the reader will not see there is the path by which he came to this coherent perspective or the motivation for pursuing it; I hope to give some sense of both by beginning with the earliest of Schafer's work related to narrative. (There is a significant body of work preceding this which is not covered here.) No strict chronology is possible because of Schafer's accretive style of working; talks and papers published in journals are revised, often drastically, then published as chapters of books. *Retelling a Life*, for example, contains material originally published almost twenty years before but substantially revised. Nevertheless, a line of development is discernible and enhances an understanding of Schafer's views.

Schafer's work on narrative grew out of his work on action language, a concept he developed in a series of papers during the early 1970s. Revised versions of those papers and additional material was gathered in *A New Language for Psychoanalysis* (1976). There and in *Language and Insight* (1978), Schafer formulated detailed and precise rules for action language. The idea is deceptively simple.

> We shall regard each psychological process, event, experience, or behavior as some kind of activity, henceforth to be called action, and shall designate each action by an active verb stating its nature and by an adverb (or adverbial locution), when applicable, stating the mode of this action. (1976, p. 9)

All else follows from this fundamental rule. Human activity should be described with verbs rather than nouns, and they should be active verbs, rather than passive or linking verbs that obscure what is happening. In this new language, "It makes me feel happy" becomes "I think of it happily" (1976, pp. 11-12). Schafer's new language focuses strictly on the question "What is a given person *doing*?" and treats as action all mental acts, including wishes, beliefs, unconscious thoughts and the experience of all emotions.

Schafer does not yet use the term "narrative," yet one can see how action language leads toward it. Our lives, even our minds' lives, become a series of identifiable actions; each action becomes part of a chain or group, and the logical thing to call each group is narrative. And even in this early work on action language, Schafer wrote of psychoanalytic life histories in ways that suggest the concerns of narrative. For example, his remark that "clinical psychoanalysis is an interpretive discipline whose concern it is to construct life histories of human beings" (1978, p. 6) emphasizes the essential narrative issues of construction (a story is created and does not exist as unalterable fact) and interpretation (a story is a product of both teller and hearer.)

Schafer refers to action language only occasionally in his later work, yet the concept reveals the drive behind much of his later thought and suggests its direction. Action language was originally offered as part of a challenge to traditional Freudian metapsychology and the assumptions behind it. Schafer objected to Freud's "establishing a mental science on the model of the natural sciences of the late nineteenth century," and to the language associated with that effort, "the quasi-physiochemical and quasi-biological language of energy, force, mechanism, structure, function, and the like" (1976, p. 362). Action language was the tool Schafer developed to reconceptualize theory; it promised a frame of observable phenomena (actions) vs. hypothetical abstractions and encouraged the use of ordinary rather than theory-laden language. To think in terms of action, and action only, prevents us from speculating about "propulsive entities" (drives) and "hypothetical substantive entities" that carry out functions like machines (1976, p. 14). Action language forces us to examine our unstated assumptions.

The tone of Schafer's work during this period is appropriately challenging and confrontive, given that the challenge he was posing seemed a more radical one in the context of the early seventies than it does now. Often his application of action language's rules seems rigid, for which he makes no apologies: "And we shall have to develop and apply this codification tirelessly and unflinchingly; for, if we do not obey the rules, we shall not really know or speak the language, and in the end we shall not have a single, coherent world to be psychoanalytic about" (1976, p. 6). Even in this early, strictly speaking "pre-narrative" phase, Schafer's work is linked to the theoretical challenges that will continue to be associated with narrative and to the problem of verifiability and coherence.

There are also clinical ideas embedded in action language. Two seem most important for understanding how Schafer will interpret narrative; both involve issues of passivity and agency. First, if all psychological processes and experience are to be expressed as actions, who is the actor? Agency and ascription of agency, an action in itself, become critical issues.

> . . . the analysand is progressively discovering, and the analyst is progressively making it plain to the analysand, not only *that* but *how* he or she is the agent or is not the agent . . . . The analysand's ascriptions of agency are reviewed, sorted out, revised, and reorganized; often, they are organized for the first time. (1978, p. 183)

Schafer writes of claimed and disclaimed actions. The proverbial "slip of the tongue" for which the speaker denies any meaning or intent is a simple example of disclaimed action. As the analysand works to claim and understand the intention behind the slip, Schafer asks us to claim, by putting into action language, all our conscious and unconscious thoughts, wishes, beliefs, and feelings. He points out that sometimes we falsely claim action, attributing to ourselves that which others have done, but that such false claiming is also action which becomes part of the narrative. Schafer's narratives emphasize recognition and experience of agency.

The other critical idea is that the performer of the actions is always a unitary person. The conception of one part of the self acting upon another part of the self fosters passivity and distracts from the complexity of the action. To say "I was struck by the thought . . . " or "overcome by feeling" is to disclaim action and avoid consideration of complex agency. In essays in *Language and Insight* (1978), Schafer discusses the concepts of self-control, self-love, and self-hate, all of which he rejects. Action language is an attempt to move away from such reflexive concepts, and the split selves implied by them, because they are part of the quasi-mechanical legacy of Freudian metapsychology. Agency replaces mechanistic parts, and so action language becomes Schafer's interpretive lens for narrative as well as the route by which he comes to the subject.

Schafer moves into full engagement with narrative in what could be called the second phase of his work–the papers published in the late seventies and early eighties, many of which were gathered in *The Analytic Attitude* (1983). He uses the term "narrative" and associated ideas to illuminate so many different aspects of psychoanalysis (technical, clinical, theoretical) that no single application of the idea to the field emerges. What follows will suggest something of its range and is ordered roughly chronologically.

In "The Appreciative Analytic Attitude and the Construction of Multiple Histories" (1979), Schafer explores the puzzle of the unitary agent experiencing and telling multiple histories. The analysand may act unconsciously, conflictually, even contradictorily, but must be engaged as a single person in order to bring forth multiple histories. Schafer begins with the supposition that there can be "no single, all purpose life history" (p. 13), because the life history will change as it is told increasingly insightfully and precisely during the course of the analysis. The life history will also change in response to the different contexts in which it appears; as the questions change, so will the history that provides the answers. Furthermore, none of these versions of the life history will be obliterated by its successor; all the versions remain, varying in power and importance as the relationships among them shift (pp. 14-15).

Schafer accepts easily but not lightly this potentially bewildering multiplicity and also accepts that different analytic approaches will produce entirely different "sets of self-confirming life histories" (p. 15). The question of how to choose among these histories or even value them he answers clearly: it is the history of the analysis itself, rather than any single version of the life history, that is of most value, because the history of the analysis includes all the other histories, is the most multiple of all the multiple histories. But he puts some fences around this inclusivity:

> That no history is the single and final one does not mean that each history is a mythic creation which is exempt from the rules of verification, coherence, consistency and (for the time being) completeness. (p. 17)

It is characteristic of Schafer to bound the idea of ever expanding multiplicity and shore it up with firm standards of verification, consistency, etc.

In "Narration in the Psychoanalytic Dialogue" (republished as a chapter in *The Analytic Attitude* and quoted here in that form), Schafer redefines most aspects of psychoanalysis in terms of narrative. In the first section of the paper Schafer redefines psychoanalytic theories as narratives. The Freudian, natural science model of psychoanalysis, the traditional metapsychology Schafer challenged with his ideas about action language, is now merely the end product of two narrative structures—Freud's view of the young child as beast and his view of the mind as a machine. (Both of these are more metaphorical than narrative, but Schafer does not address that.) Schafer now views these narratives as possible structures to be adopted but cites the work of Melanie Klein and Kohut as alternative narrative structures to be considered.

Schafer turns from theory to how narration functions in the psychoanalytic dialogue itself. The dialogue is entirely a matter of narrative. The analysand tells of himself and thereby makes a self, and he tells of others and thereby makes them. Selves are "constituted by narrative actions," and "we narrate others just as we narrate ourselves" (p. 219). In making interpretations, the analyst is retelling the analysand's story and reshaping it in ways the analysand incorporates into his further tellings, so the end result is "an interweaving of texts" and a "jointly authored work" (p. 219). The narrative developed is psychoanalytic in nature because it is focused on transference and resistance.

Yet those concepts too are narrative structures subject to revision, which Schafer does in the later part of the paper. For example, he challenges the passive narrative implication of our usual view of resistance, and offers instead three possible interpretations of resistance that affirm the analysand's potential for agency. Similarly, he criticizes the traditional view of free association as one encouraging passive, disclaiming narrative and offers an alternative in which the analysand is the active constructor of narrative and the analyst focuses on the telling, not the material passively revealed. Schafer also challenges the concept of the normative life history, showing that the competing theories of development and the research used to prove them are only the imposition of certain preconceived narrative structures. They constitute "second order" histories while the first order history is the story of the analytic dialogue itself, the process of telling and retelling. In contrast to the normative life history's explanation and recreation of past events, for Schafer, "The time is always the present. The event is always an ongoing dialogue" (p. 239).

With this essay, Schafer reconceptualizes the whole field of psychoanalysis in terms of narrative and so risks using the term excessively globally. If everything is narrative, the term points to nothing in particular and ceases to be useful. In other essays he sharpens his focus on the particular and avoids the danger. He turns to the particulars of theory–how it is developed, used, and confirmed–in *Narrative Actions in Psychoanalysis* (1981). It is a small, dense book, impossible, at least for this reviewer, to summarize intelligibly. What can easily and most usefully be noted is the nature of the arguments; this book most clearly shows Schafer's attraction to and work with literary theory. The book consists of two chapters–"Narratives of Space" and "Narratives of Time"–and both are much more about metaphor, its nature and implications, than about narrative *per se*. Schafer's reference list includes poets, art historians, literary critics, and a half dozen philosophers noted for their work in the philosophy of language. In this context, Schafer's methods of validation change. Standards of consistency and coherence are replaced with an acceptance that all understanding is circular and that there can be no absolute distinction between finding and hypothesis (p. 15). Most significantly, he adopts hermeneutic theory as an appropriate and productive frame for an interpretive discipline. Elsewhere he tells us his work "amounts to a hermeneutic version of psychoanalysis" (1983, p. 255).

A less theoretical literary aspect of Schafer appears in "Action and Narration in Psychoanalysis," first published in *New Literary History* and then in *The Analytic Attitude* (1983). Schafer's aim here is to show how " . . . the narrative being composed and the subjective world being constituted may be inferred from the analysand's language and its context" (p. 243). Translating disclaiming language into action language, Schafer explains the different worlds so described. "The edge of a doubt began to intrude itself" becomes "I am beginning to doubt the truth of what I just said. (The subject attributes no spatial extension and motion to thoughts.)" "I can't escape the feeling that it won't work" becomes "I continue to think that it won't work, and I wish I didn't think of it in that dismal way. (The speaker is not now beset by implicitly persecutory feelings)" (pp. 246-247). Schafer's aim here seems to be to show us how to interpret a text, what principles to use, what language to look for. His use of narrative is firmly grounded and clinically based. He is doing something very like the close textual analysis literary critics, as opposed to literary theorists, engage in.

Another literary side of Schafer's interests is seen in "The Imprisoned Analysand," a chapter of *The Analytic Attitude* (1983). Schafer describes the kind of stories analysts should be prepared to listen for and explains how they can use their narrative competence–their knowledge of the culture's stories, their own daydreams and analytic training (p. 260)–to enhance their work. He uses the term "storyline," richly mingling elements of narrative structure, theme, and metaphor, and lists several of the most evocative ones–the journey, the trial, the phoenix, Cinderella, the exile, the odyssey (p. 259). But it is the story of imprisonment with which he is most concerned. Schafer describes many different ways the narrative can be presented and experienced by the analysand and different ways it can be heard by the analyst. Most of all he shows how over the course of an analysis attentive to narrative redevelopment, the story can be changed and a new freedom achieved.

> The new freedom . . . will be that of a readiness to entertain multiple and less acutely conflictual possibilities of understanding and, along with these, multiple possibilities of feeling, revaluation, and action in the world. But in another and equally important respect, the narrative redevelopment of the case leads to the analysand's seeing the prison in a new and happier light, that is, seeing it also as one of the expectable, unconsciously developed narratives of committing oneself steadfastly to personal aims, values, and human relationships. (pp. 280-281)

In the first narrative redevelopment, freedom seems to be synonymous with the exercise of agency. In the second, the happier view of the prison seems to come from a willingness to accept responsibility for and make a commitment to one's own actions. Rather than one part of the self imprisoning another, a unitary self intentionally designs a satisfying commitment. Schafer's interpretations of narrative are still and ultimately rooted in action language.

Retelling a Life (1992) gathers many of Schafer's later papers and some of his much earlier work as well. He develops and refines many of his arguments about the nature of narrative and its place in psychoanalysis. Along the way he clarifies many issues, for example, his use of the term "storyline." The term seemed murky, if rich, in "The Imprisoned Analysand." Schafer now explains exactly what he means by the term and why it is preferable to other closely linked concepts (see chapters 2 and 3). Often these clarifications of terms and issues seem to be responses to criticism his work has encountered, and in addressing them he addresses other areas of work in psychoanalysis and broadens the context of his ideas, letting us see them in the perspective of the field as a whole. Schafer enhances his ideas on narrative in this latest book and enriches them with many clinical examples, but he does not substantially add to them. The one notable addition to his work in the book is the section on gender issues (some revised and some new material), a welcome and valuable contribution but not particularly related to narrative issues.

Still, *Retelling a Life* is different enough to be considered a third phase of work, and the difference is perhaps most usefully described in terms of tone or argumentative stance. Schafer takes up the themes that have always permeated his work and reflects upon them rather than arguing for them. For instance, in the chapter "Self-deception, Defense, and Narration," Schafer puzzles again over the relation of multiple narratives of self and unitary agency. He explains why he took the stance he did in previous work and tells us that he continues to "favor" that position but with the full understanding that other positions are possible. Given that others are possible, Schafer must justify his choice, and this brings him back to another pervasive theme of his work, the problem of validation: How does one choose one narrative over another? He answers simply that the "single-person program seems to have an important heuristic advantage" (p. 51). In other words, that narrative is best which provokes the most speculation and investigation. But by the end of the article he is still grappling with the question and cites, as he has in his earlier works, standards of "consistency, coherence, comprehensiveness, and common sense." But these now seem less determinative, and less easily determinable.

> But in the complex instances that concern us the most, we cannot count on incontestable proofs of superiority and we resort to, or submit to, rhetorical, ethical, and esthetic persuasiveness to decide what is better or best. (p. 56)

There is a flexibility here, perhaps even humility, which seems a long way from Schafer's absolute insistence in *A New Language* that rules of action language be applied rigorously and consistently because failure to do so will destroy the possibility of having "a single, coherent world to be psychoanalytic about" (1976, p. 6).

This new openness and inclusivity is particularly evident in Schafer's chapters on theory. His remarks there make it very clear that there is no "single, coherent world" anymore, and yet Schafer's views do not seem to have changed essentially, only expanded. What Schafer previously treated as a single, traditional, Freudian metapsychology he now revisits, describing it as multiple Freudian legacies, a pluralistic view "forever subject to change" (p. 154) but always rich in meaning to every new generation of readers. Schafer's earlier tone of challenge and confrontation is no longer necessary, because traditional Freudian metapsychology no longer dominates the field, rather Schafer's own ideas and those related to them are at the center now. But that can be true only if there is still a center, a question Schafer addresses in his remarks on the search for common ground in comparative psychoanalysis. These will be discussed in relation to Donald Spence's views on the subject.

DONALD SPENCE'S CONTRIBUTIONS TO NARRATIVE

Schafer came to the subject of narrative gradually, as part of a study of interpretive questions. Spence begins with narrative, introducing in *Narra-*

tive Truth and Historical Truth (1982) the essential ideas that will continue to inform his work on interpretation and finding meaning.

Spence presents two major and somewhat contradictory ideas in this book. The first two thirds of the book describe the extent to which narrative is and has always been an intrinsic part of the analytic process and its reporting. Memory, language, and experience of analyst and analysand tend to shape experience into comprehensible patterns which can be construed as narratives. In the realm of reporting, Spence argues that Freud established the tradition of selectively reporting the details of cases to emphasize particular points, and the profession has followed his example to the extent that there is nearly habitual indulgence in narrative construction which may bear no resemblance to what actually happened, and, more seriously, no awareness of any discrepancy. In the final third of the book Spence decries this state of affairs and calls for the systematic "naturalizing" or "unpacking" of the text of the therapeutic hour within moments of its end so that there is a record of what actually happened, rather than what the analyst thought happened. Such unpacking will provide the data necessary for a firmer theoretical base for psychoanalysis.

The two ideas do not sit together easily. The problem of the field containing and using both is evident in Spence's definition of terms. Note that he defines not narrative or history, but their respective truths.

> Narrative truth can be defined as the criterion we use to decide when a certain experience has been captured to our satisfaction; it depends on continuity and closure and the extent to which the fit of the pieces takes on an aesthetic finality. . . . Once a given construction has acquired narrative truth, it becomes just as real as any other kind of truth. (p. 31)

> Historical truth is time-bound and is dedicated to the strict observance of correspondence rules; our aim is to come as close as possible to what "really" happened. Historical truth is not satisfied with coherence for its own sake; we must have assurance that the pieces being fitted into the puzzle also belong to a certain time and place and that this belonging can be corroborated in some systematic manner. (p. 32)

The contrast seems to be between aesthetic validation and objective or "scientific" validation. Spence's emphasis is entirely upon validity and how it can be determined. The comparative value of the truths is not considered, and neither history nor narrative is seen as a means of exploration or a way of adding or refining questions about what we do not know. What matters to Spence is what we do know and whether we can prove it.

Spence is deeply interested in problems of communication. He gives serious attention to the problems of putting human experience into words and understanding that experience from the words. He explores those problems in his chapters "Putting Things into Words" and "Putting Pictures into Words" by examining how we receive information from literary texts and paintings. Spence argues that a literary text and a clinical hour are analogous in that they both require what he calls constructive listening. Evenly hovering attention is inadequate to the complexity of free association which "to be understood in any depth, requires a certain kind of active and constructive listening in which the analyst is continually supplying meanings, choosing from a range of ambiguities, and, in general, imposing his own context on the material" (p. 53). The less freely the patient associates the more neutrally the analyst can listen, so the concepts of evenly hovering attention and free association are not in a symmetrical relation as Freud argued but a reciprocal relation (p. 53). Turning to visual data, Spence is particularly thought provoking, arguing that much of the primary data of analysis is visual (preverbal memories, sensory experiences or dreams), and that there is no language adequate to convey visual experience.

These problems of transmission and reception of information result in what Spence calls "unwitting interpretations"–"the background assumptions necessary for the process of understanding" (p. 34). Both patient and analyst shape the analytic process with their unwitting interpretations, and Spence considers both sides. From the patient's side he describes the working of memory and how memory can be influenced by suggestion, citing Loftus' experiments which quantify the ways memory is vulnerable to a wide range of interfering stimuli. Memory can also be distorted by language: " . . . the very act of talking about the past tends to crystallize it in specific but somewhat arbitrary language, and this language serves, in turn, to distort the early memory" (p. 92). The form of the description tends to replace the memory. Transferential issues, the patient's sense of the context he is addressing, also shape recall.

The analyst's constructive listening is perhaps the more significant source of unwitting interpretations. He listens "with a focus already sharpened by theory" (p. 100), and "registration inevitably becomes interpretation" (p. 102). Spence highlights the principles governing analytic listening, the assumptions determining the nature of the constructive listening. Most important is the search after meaning.

This has become the analyst's stock in trade. He prides himself on bringing meaning out of chaos; he often feels uncomfortable with persisting ambiguity and finds it difficult to admit to himself that there may be no unifying theme, no simple solution to increasingly complex material. (p. 107)

The nature of the meaning being sought is largely predetermined by what Spence calls the "conventions of psychoanalytic understanding" (p. 109). Analysts listen for thematic unity. They assume that there is significant therapeutic meaning in any material being discussed (the convention of therapeutic urgency). Their listening is also governed by the principle of multiple function, the convention of transference and the convention of empathic listening. Spence demonstrates that these principles determined Freud's reporting of the Wolf Man case, and he analyzes the Grusha incident to show that it is a narrative construction based on the conventions above rather than an objectively retrieved memory or reconstructed moment of the past. Spence shows how "supposition has become assertion" and facts are invented by "evidential need" (p. 119). He further argues that this predetermined, constructive listening will affect the material revealed by the patient. A circle of unwitting interpretations creating more unwitting interpretations begins to emerge.

Spence's rather negative attitude to narrative reconstruction changes when he turns to formal interpretations. The narrative reconstructions of unwitting interpretations were suspect because they diverted attention from or falsified historical truth, but Spence views narrative's role in formal interpretations quite differently.

When we make a formal interpretation, we are finding a narrative home for an anomalous happening. We are using language to clothe this event in respectability and take away some of its strangeness and mystery, and by fitting the language into the patient's life story, we are giving it a narrative home. The linguistic and narrative aspects of an interpretation may well have priority over its historical truth. . . . (p. 137)

Spence illustrates these ideas with a specimen interpretation which he presents as historically dubious but nevertheless compelling and then turns to the interesting question of what makes such an interpretation compelling. Historical truth is not the criterion of a good interpretation, rather qualities which contribute to narrative truth are those that compel. He lists three criteria, three rules governing narrative truth. The rule of clinical parsimony posits that the smallest explanation that can account for the largest number of facts is preferable. Second is the rule that similarity of form suggests similarity of content, that external form is a clue to inner meaning. Finally, there is the rule that pattern matches–correspondences between past and present events in a patient's life–indicate cause and effect (pp. 144-145).

It is very difficult to determine Spence's attitude to these rules and the consequences of applying them in formal interpretation. He painstakingly shows that each of these rules falsifies clinical data and encourages analytic hyperingenuity of the most suspect sort. Clinical parsimony allows us to ignore inconvenient facts; no modern form of thought persuades that inner meaning is expressed in external form, and pattern matches are all too easily found–usually based on "a clever application of language to a pair of random events" (p. 157) and almost never indicating even a plausible cause and effect relation. Nevertheless, these are the rules governing a "good" interpretation.

Spence tries to resolve this apparent contradiction by arguing that a good interpretation takes advantage of the flexibility of language and chooses (by unannounced principles) "which of several linguistic formulations to emphasize" (p. 163). And so Spence makes his dramatic point that "the analyst functions much more as a poet than as a historian" (p. 164). Citing the work of Loch and Viderman, Spence concludes that "all interpretations are inexact to a greater or lesser extent" and that language gives us the power to "exchange one kind of truth–historical truth–for the truth of being coherent and sayable–narrative truth" (p. 173).

A similar ambivalence about the power and role of narrative is evident as Spence continues his argument by explaining that "something may become true simply by being put into words" (p. 175). He continues to advance the idea of creative interpretation as an attempt "to bring separate ideas together in a new and potentially evocative combination" (p. 178) and quotes Ricoeur on the goal of raising "case history to the sort of narrative intelligibility we ordinarily expect from a story" (p. 179). To this extent narrative seems to be a positive force in analysis and case reporting, and Spence explains how the degree of narrative fit determines the degree of credence given an interpretation. But then the terms shift from credence to validation:

> As metapyschology has tended to come under attack, clinical reasoning, as represented in clinical reports, tends to depend more and more on narrative fit. The aesthetic quality of the case history has tended, as a result, to pre-empt the use of general law. Narrative truth has tended to supplant historical truth. (p. 186)

This begins to sound dangerous, and Spence suggests there is something insidious in narrative truths. A creative interpretation "takes on a special kind of grace and is automatically granted a kind of privileged status," and he cautions us that the two truths should always be kept distinct (p. 187), though he doesn't tell us how that would be possible. Dichotomizing truths, he argues that narrative truth is inadequate to the building of theory and general law. The field needs firmer evidence, historical truth, for such building.

With this argument Spence is well into the other major point of the book, that the field of psychoanalysis needs far more, and far more systematic, research. The argument begins simply. Spence distinguishes between normative psychoanalytic competence, that belonging to all trained members of the community, and privileged psychoanalytic competence, that belonging to "the analyst at a specific time and place in a particular analysis" (p. 216). The aim of the research Spence proposes is to make the knowledge of privileged competence part of the permanent record available to all those with normative competence. A tape recording of sessions is insufficient for this purpose because it is too often unintelligible, and even verbatim transcripts corrected by the analyst fail to provide enough information. What Spence wants are the private commentaries of the analyst and the full context of the interchanges which they should provide.

These private commentaries of the clinical hour are what constitute for Spence "the fully naturalized text." Here the role of narrative complicates the nature of the research Spence proposes.

> Naturalization becomes an essential step in filling out the record and in providing the necessary context by which the seemingly random bits and pieces of the patient's behavior begin to make sense. Naturalization is a necessary consequence of the fact that we depend heavily on a narrative form of explanation and that parts of the narrative can be supplied only by the treating analyst. (p. 219)

These naturalizations seem to be the analyst's private interpretation of the narrative he has perceived, and Spence has astoundingly high expectations for the knowledge to be gained from these glosses. They will make the difference between knowing and experiencing the clinical hour (p. 217) and will "explicate all ambiguities" (p. 228). Further, "a proper gloss would make explicit the meaning of every observation, and it would make it possible to name its elements without first assuming an interpretation" (p. 246).

Is such "unpacking" possible? Spence tells us the answer to that question is crucial, more important than "whether psychoanalysis is a science or a pseudo science or whether the treatment is real or a placebo." The crucial question for Spence is whether we have even "the beginnings of a shared discipline" (p. 243). But the answer is complicated by Spence's contradictory views of narrative, its nature and value.

Spence is not naive about the difficulties of naturalization. If the unpacking is to provide an accurate reconstruction rather than merely a plausible account, reporting analysts will have to suspend their preference for coherence and continuity (p. 247). In short, they will have to learn to become historians rather than conventional narrators. Even posing such a requirement, Spence realizes he is back to the problem of how to put things into words or "to what might be called the problem of narrative technique" (p. 249). Rather than retreating into a simplistic view of objective history, Spence pushes the argument the other way and, again, demands poetic skill from analysts. " . . . some way must be found to artistically rearrange the material to produce a new account . . . that will dramatize the relevant issues and supply the necessary ground against which the actual utterances are heard" (p. 250). Such an account will even have to be sensitive to the nuances of language and metaphor (pp. 256-260).

On the other hand, this artistic creation will be judged by standards that seem utterly alien to its mode.

> . . . the naturalized vignette can be evaluated by the effect it achieves. If it brings to the outside reader the kind of inevitable persuasion that we have learned to associate with a classic philosophical argument or mathematical proof, then we have achieved our goal of making privileged data publicly accessible. (p. 262)

Neither historical nor narrative truth offers such compelling argument, so implicitly Spence has answered his question–negatively. If complete unpacking is the only acceptable form of publicly available systematic research, then we have not even the "beginning of a shared discipline."

Spence is an optimist, however, and perseveres, undaunted by this apparent dead end. He returns to a theme running throughout the book of Freud's recurring metaphor of psychoanalysis as an archeology which reconstructs a past from fragments buried in the mind. Throughout the book, Spence has rejected that model because of its emphasis solely on historical truth and its theoretical rejection of the narrative tradition even while relying on narrative means. The archeological model treats narrative constructions like genuine reconstructions of the past, treats narrative truth as if it were synonymous with historical truth, and so achieves no truth at all. Furthermore, the model obscures some of the genuine truth available to us, offering "a kind of misplaced concreteness that does an injustice to the verbal utterance" (p. 267). Spence again rejects the model with its emphasis on fragment finding and argues that it be replaced with an artistic model.

> In defining an interpretation as either a pragmatic statement [one designed solely for its effect] or an artistic creation, we are emphasizing the fact that its truth value is contingent. By definition, therefore, an interpretation can no longer be evaluated in its singular propositional form but must be considered with respect to the conditions under which it was expressed (created) and the outcome it produced. (pp. 276-7)

Spence's demands have become less stringent; he is willing to allow for contingency in a way that philosophical and mathematical proof do not permit. Most important, he returns to the nature of the verbal utterances comprising an analysis, the verbal surface with all the attendant problems of interpreting language. As a result, he returns too to the problem of unpacking or naturalization. Even if it is impossible, it must be attempted.

> We have exchanged the problem of finding answers in the past–the archeological model–for the equally difficult problem of naturalizing the present. . . . we have no choice but to make it fully explicit. (p. 278)

Even with the acceptance of contingency and the complexity of verbal surface, one wonders at Spence's assurance about the prospect of making anything, much less the complexities of the analytic space, fully explicit.

The essential contradiction in Spence's attitude toward the value of narrative truth was succinctly described in a review of the book by Sass and Woolfoolk.

> . . . the first two thirds of the book argue that, in the typical psychoanalytic interpretation, the demands of coherence ("narrative truth") largely overwhelm those of correspondence ("historical truth"), yet this does not significantly diminish the therapeutic impact of these interpretations. When Spence comes to the *scientific* situation, however, he takes precisely the opposite position. . . . Spence seems to see something very like historical truth not only as possible, but as the sole possible saviour of the validity of psychological knowledge. (1988, pp. 445-6)

There is also a poignancy to the contradiction, because it points to competing needs. In the final pages of the book Spence is still grappling with the conflict: " . . . narrative truth is the source of our clinical success," but we still very much need a "science of the mind" (pp. 296-7). He is unable to relinquish either narrative knowing or scientific knowing, and he cannot bring them together.

The attempt to resolve the apparent conflict animates much of Spence's later work. He eventually drops the term "narrative" and seems to switch positions on several crucial issues, but his concern remains the same: If meaning of whatever sort is made, not found, how do we know we can trust it? In this, of course, he is posing the same question Schafer addressed repeatedly in his work: Which narrative do we choose and why?

In his second book, *The Freudian Metaphor* (1987), Spence reconceptualizes his concern in terms of metaphor and addresses the nature of theory building. He begins with the supposition that no neutral theory is possible since all theory is built on metaphor which by its nature resists falsification; metaphor can be displaced but not disproved. The purpose of the book is partly to sensitize readers to the metaphorical basis of the Freudian system so that they can recognize its limitations:

> It is not a lawful set of axioms which calls for explicit testing . . . . It might even be argued that calls for such testing represent a serious literalization of the Freudian metaphor and a mistaken belief that the critical psychoanalytic concepts possess a testable reality. (p. 7)

Since all theory, not only Freudian theory, is based on metaphor, no scientific testing is possible. This is a far cry from Spence's previous insistence upon building a body of hard data to rescue psychoanalysis from the danger of pseudo-science.

Spence has not left the subject of narrative behind him entirely. The archeological model described and rejected in *Narrative Truth and Historical Truth*, in which analysis is seen as uncovering literal bits of historical fact, now becomes "the Sherlock Holmes tradition." The therapist/sleuth confronts disconnected events/symptoms in the life of the client/patient, with a dispassionate trust that careful analysis of the facts will reveal a truth that explains all with a single stroke (p. 114). Spence argues that this tradition is the basis of all case reporting; it is the storyline that analysts learned from Freud and mindlessly replicate. He rejects it as being completely inadequate to the complexities of the analytic situation, which of course it is. What is instructive in this is that in Spence's on-going conflict between narrative and factual or scientific ways of knowing, he consistently focuses on naive and reductive versions of narrative. It is as if he is simultaneously intrigued by and wary of the multiplicity of meaning that narrative can bring to the field and so strictly circumscribes it (chooses narrow, limited, simplistic narratives), thereby guaranteeing that the narrative basis of knowing will be rejected.

Narrative is rejected, but what of science? Spence reverses his position dramatically when he rejects psychoanalysis as a science. In *The Freudian Metaphor* he emphatically proves that the methodology of the field meets none of the requirements of scientific validity. To make his point, Spence refutes the work of Brenner and Holt and in so doing describes well the reluctance to give up the idea of a true, scientific underpinning to psychoanalytic work. There is something "enormously comforting" (p. 75) in the idea of scientific validity, and he describes psychoanalysis's "unceasing quest for scientific status" as a desire for "the right to join the *better half* [italics added] of C. P. Snow's two cultures" (p. 71).

Rejecting narrative and scientific possibilities of validation in psychoanalysis, Spence comes to hermeneutics, the apparent resolution to the conflict his work has been addressing. For hermeneutics to provide such resolution it must allow for the richness and complexity of narrative and also be publicly available, systematic and verifiable. In the section of *The Freudian Metaphor* titled "The Metaphor of Psychoanalysis as Science" and in his contribution to a book on hermeneutics (Spence, 1988), Spence outlines his quite particular version of hermeneutics. It is noteworthy that in the process he recreates something very like the conflict between narrative and historical truth. He develops the concepts of tough and tender minded hermeneutics–tender minded, those based on soft pattern matches and the assumption of readily discoverable deep-seated lawfulness; tough minded, those based on the assumption of randomness until proven otherwise, what Spence calls the "Know-Nothing world view." As a staunch advocate of tough minded hermeneutics, Spence conceives of the null position.

> The null position demands relentless suspicion of all possible contaminating conditions, a skeptical attitude which doubts all findings until they are replicated and/or independently arrived at, and a steadfast openness to new discoveries and new findings. (1987, p. 211)

Spence sounds suspiciously like those he described before whose desperation to prove psychoanalysis was a science (and not a hermeneutic and interpretive discipline) came from their horror of losing the comfort of scientific validity. But instead of affirming the scientific basis of psychoanalysis, Spence invents a scientific hermeneutics.

In this later work (see also "The Rhetorical Voice of Psychoanalysis," 1990) Spence has notably revised his positions, yet the later work still seems more consistent with than divergent from the ideas in *Narrative*

Truth and Historical Truth. There has, however, been one significant shift in the sort of systematic research to be undertaken. Spence sensibly retreats from the idea of a complete unpacking of a text of a clinical hour which will make all meaning "fully explicit." He proposes instead that psychoanalysis develop its archives (data base) as the legal field does. He argues that law and psychoanalysis progress in a similar manner, applying general laws to specific situations with the understanding that the specific situation will in turn modify and redefine the general law. Spence proposes a system of peer commentary, invited commentary on specimen texts which will eventually accumulate into a complex body of knowledge. Case reports, the nature of which Spence severely criticized before, now need be no more than "approximations of a very complex truth" (1987, p. 174), which presumably the accumulation will ultimately provide. In this new model, "wisdom emerges from the gradual accumulation of differing readings of the same situations and the accumulating overlay of new contexts" (p. 179). One may argue with the details of the analogy of law and psychoanalysis, but this is a far more reasonable way to proceed with systematic research.

A COMPARISON AND CONCLUSION

Schafer and Spence are alike in addressing clinical and theoretical issues in terms of narrative. They explore how meaning is made in the clinical hour, in case reporting, and in publication, as well as at the theoretical level with a focus on narrative, metaphor and storyline. They are perhaps most alike in conceiving of any given theory as one of several possible storylines; beyond that they use narrative markedly differently. Spence drops the term after his first book, though he continues to work with closely related concepts. Schafer develops the term, refining and enhancing its use particularly at the clinical level. Spence's interest seemed primarily in identifying narratives and proving they were narratives rather than facts. Schafer stays with the narratives, exploring their nature and implications.

Beyond the narrow focus on narrative, on questions of how psychoanalytic meaning is made and the nature of the psychoanalytic discipline, Schafer and Spence have moved closer together over the course of their work. In challenging the traditional Freudian metapsychology, they have both adopted the position that psychoanalysis is not a science but an interpretive discipline. Once Schafer relaxes his insistence that we literally and exclusively use action language, he adopts the interpretive position easily, embracing the multiplicity and tolerating the uncertainty of narrative ways of thinking. Spence's move seems much more conflicted, more reluctant, and the problems it raises continue to dominate his work. The differences between Schafer and Spence are now in their conceptions of the interpretive discipline, and there is still a great deal of room for divergence.

The situation can usefully be seen in a recent issue of the *International Journal of Psycho-Analysis*, a thematically organized issue gathering writers on the topics of conceptualization and communication of clinical facts in psychoanalysis–topics central to the ideas of Schafer and Spence, both of whom contribute to the issue. I noted above that Schafer's tone changes over the course of his work (the challenging, confrontive stance of the early work on narrative is replaced with a more open, inclusive position) and suggested the change might be attributable to the fact that Schafer's ideas and those related to them are now more at the center of the field. The concept of a center presents too precise and orderly an image, however. The gathering represented by this issue of *IJPA* is more reflective of the range and strains of the field, and so even within this gathering of common concerns Schafer and Spence maintain their characteristic differences.

Spence (1994) is still concerned with the differences between scientific and psychoanalytic facts and the difficulties of achieving a "secure and accumulating knowledge base" (p. 917). He accepts that most facts are socially constructed but instead of exploring how and why he works to establish a different sort of fact, he calls them "latent facts," that have the "potential for both greater reliability and greater falsifiability than the average clinical fact" (p. 923). He is still searching for "underlying lawfulness . . . and a common market currency that will translate readily from one brand of psychoanalysis to another" (p. 924). For Schafer all facts, without exception, are conceptualized and to become a clinical fact an observation must be yet further reconceptualized. Even such reconceptualized facts should be accepted only provisionally and temporarily until they are replaced by new narrative lines. The closest Schafer comes to underlying lawfulness is his claim that "facticity must remain in flux"–"Facts presented as permanently fixed should be viewed with suspicion" (1994, p. 1024).

Even the ways these theorists search for common ground differ. Spence looks for generalized and generalizable findings, the common market currency that can be readily translated. In *Retelling a Life* Schafer claims it is impossible to work, write or publish in the field without a systematic bias. He argues that in the study of comparative psychoanalytic theory we should look for differences rather than similarities and generalizability and that the conflict thus generated will bring more self awareness and creativity (1992, pp. 191-192). He warns that the search for singleness and uniformity (both implied by Spence's "common currency") will stifle growth in the field of psychoanalysis. Schafer's concern, shown here, for multiplicity of narratives is consistent with his work and is one of its most valuable aspects, but his warning against singleness seems irrelevant. Some agreement has been achieved in the lines of thought traced in these two writers: traditional Freudian metapsychology (however that may have been conceptualized and may be now reconceptualized) has been superseded, but the work of Schafer and Spence show how varied the progress of the field can be beyond that agreement.

REFERENCES

Sass, Louis A. & Woolfolk, Robert. L. (1988). Psychoanalysis and the hermeneutic turn: A critique of *Narrative truth and historical truth. Journal of the American Psychoanalytic Association, 36*(2), 429-454.

Schafer, R. (1976). *A new language for psychoanalysis*. New Haven: Yale University Press.

Schafer, R. (1978). *Language and insight*. New Haven: Yale University Press.

Schafer, R. (1979). The appreciative analytic attitude and the construction of multiple histories. *Psychoanalysis and Contemporary Thought, 2*, 3-24.

Schafer, R. (1981). *Narrative actions in psychoanalysis*. Worcester, MA: Clark University Press.

Schafer, R. (1983). *The analytic attitude*. New York: Basic Books.

Schafer, R. (1992). *Retelling a life: Narration and dialogue in psychoanalysis*. New York: Basic Books.

Schafer, R. (1994). The conceptualisation of clinical facts. *International Journal of Psycho-Analysis, 75*, 1023-1030.

Spence, Donald P. (1982). *Narrative truth and historical truth: Meaning and interpretation in psychoanalysis*. New York: W. W. Norton and Company.

Spence, Donald P. (1987). *The Freudian metaphor: Toward paradigm change in psychoanalysis*. New York: W. W. Norton.

Spence, Donald P. (1988). Tough and tender-minded hermeneutics. In S. B. Messer, L. A. Sass, & R. L. Woolfolk (Eds.), *Hermeneutics and psychological theory: Interpretive perspectives on personality, psychotherapy, and psychopathology* (pp. 62-84). New Brunswick, N J: Rutgers University Press.

Spence, Donald P. (1990). The rhetorical voice of psychoanalysis. *Journal of the American Psychoanalytic Association, 38*(3), 579-603.

Spence, Donald P. (1994). The special nature of psychoanalytic facts. *International Journal of Psycho-Analysis, 75*, 915-925.

Chapter 2

Paradigms, Metaphors, and Narratives: Stories We Tell About Development

Joseph Palombo

SUMMARY. This paper addresses the issue of the status of developmental theories. It discusses the concepts of paradigm, metaphor, and narrative as these apply to developmental theories. The author argues that all developmental theories use metaphors as explanatory models. The type of metaphor a theory uses determines whether or not it has a narrative structure. Developmental theories that use a contextual metaphor as opposed to those that use mechanistic or organismic metaphors do not have narrative structure, although their applications to individual cases create narratives. By examining the type of metaphor developmental theories use it is possible to construct a theory that is both coherent and that corresponds to the events associated with development. This conclusion leads to the rejection of constructivist approaches to viewing development, and

Joseph Palombo is Founding Dean, Institute for Clinical Social Work, Chicago; Faculty Member, Child and Adolescent Psychotherapy Program, Chicago Institute for Psychoanalysis; Research Associate, Department of Pediatrics, Rush-Presbyterian-St. Luke's Medical Center; and is in private practice.

A different version of this paper was presented at the conference "Theory Matters: A conference exploring the relationship between clinical theory and clinical practice," sponsored by the Institute for Clinical Social Work, Chicago, September 23, 1994.

[Haworth co-indexing entry note]: "Paradigms, Metaphors, and Narratives: Stories We Tell About Development." Palombo, Joseph. Co-published simultaneously in *Journal of Analytic Social Work* (The Haworth Press, Inc.) Vol. 3, No. 2/3, 1996, pp. 31-59; and: *Narration and Therapeutic Action: The Construction of Meaning in Psychoanalytic Social Work* (ed: Jerrold R. Brandell) The Haworth Press, Inc., 1996, pp. 31-59. Single or multiple copies of this article are available from The Haworth Document Delivery Service [1-800-342-9678, 9:00 a.m. - 5:00 p.m. (EST) E-mail address: get info@ haworth.com].

suggests that it is possible for a developmental theory to attain the status of a paradigm. *[Article copies available from The Haworth Document Delivery Service: 1-800-342-9678. E-mail address: getinfo@haworth.com].*

There is general agreement among psychoanalytic practitioners that developmental theories play a central role in understanding human conduct. These theories provide a conceptual framework for the relationship between past occurrences, present personality structure, and psychopathology. In addition, they are integral to the conduct of clinical practice. Since psychoanalytic clinical theories subscribe to the principles of developmental psychopathology, it is hard to conceive of a psychoanalytic clinical theory that does not include a development theory.

In previous papers, I discussed the problems clinicians face in relating their developmental theories to their clinical theories (Palombo, 1991a; 1991b). I suggested that a "chasm" exists between the two theories. This chasm appears unbridgeable given the current status of some of these theories. The chasm exists because of three different sets of problems: methodological, clinical, and theoretical. From a methodological perspective, the data that researchers on development collect is different from that collected by clinicians. Developmental theorists collect data that is directly observable and is capable of consensual validation, whereas clinicians' data consists of patients' introspective reports from which inferences are made as to the patient's experience and state of mind. From a clinical perspective therapists reconstruct past events but have no direct access to confirmatory data. Therapists use their developmental theory to organize their data and to explain what derailed a patient's development. Since there is no way to establish the external validity of these reconstructions, the premise that a relationship exists between a therapist's theory of development and the patient's productions is brought into question. The disparity in status between developmental theories and clinicians' theories results in the problems associated with what Spence called "narrative truth" and "historical truth" (Spence, 1982). Finally, researchers on development aspire to construct theories that have the status of universal paradigms, while the theories clinicians use do not lend themselves to similar generalization (Klein, 1973), as is evident from the problems of establishing a model technique in analysis or psychotherapy. Most clinical theories are themselves narratives that lead to the construction of case histories or individual narratives. Such clinical theories are not verifiable in the way that hypotheses generated by paradigms are verifiable.

Bridging this chasm requires the formulation of a unified theory of subjectivity that incorporates developmental, pathological, and curative processes. Kohut's empathic/introspective approach offers a clinical theory of the curative effects of therapy. He also formulates a broad theory of the factors that can derail development and produce disorders of the self. No equivalent developmental theory has emerged. In this paper I do not attempt to formulate such a theory; rather, I limit myself to a discussion of the means through which it would be possible to attain such a goal. This entails examining three sets of issues: (a) are developmental theories narratives or paradigms? (b) what is an appropriate metaphor for a developmental theory that deals with the subjectivity? and, (c) can this metaphor be consistent with the empathic/introspective approach?

ON PARADIGMS, NARRATIVES, AND ROOT METAPHORS

First is the question of whether developmental theories are paradigms, in the sense which I will define, or culture bound narratives that reflect the child rearing of the social/cultural group in which they are proposed. That is, are developmental theories paradigms with a set of hypotheses that articulate universal propositions about the course of development, or do they constitute "ideal types" or prototypes, based on a social/cultural group's view of a healthy individual, that serve as models on which therapists pattern their assessment of individual case histories?

There is general agreement that clinicians construct case histories, or narratives, out of patients' data. As narratives, these case histories have a protagonist, a plot, a beginning, a middle, an end, and a dramatic core that is focal in the treatment. The question is whether the construction of those narratives is guided by a developmental theory and whether the theory that guides the construction or reconstruction itself has a similar narrative structure. If the latter is the case, I will maintain that the developmental theory cannot have the status of a paradigm. I will argue that most current psychoanalytic developmental theories rely on two particular types of root metaphors to organize their data, the mechanistic and the organismic. These metaphors, while purporting to give descriptions of psychological phenomena, present a narrator's account of the phenomena as reified entities that are located spatially within the person's psyche. They suffer from the further difficulty that they cannot give insight into the person's subjective states, because they cannot consistently incorporate the personal and shared meanings of patients' experiences into their explanatory scheme. Metaphors that refer to organic or mechanical processes cannot translate human experience into its component meanings for the person.

On the other hand, the use of a different root metaphor can make possible the construction of a coherent psychoanalytic theory of development that achieves the status of a paradigm. This is the contextual metaphor that focuses on the *meaning of experience* rather than on psychological phenomena as reified objects. It is similar to the focus on the meaning of experience used in the clinical setting. When Kohut suggested the use of the empathic/introspective method as a necessary condition for understanding human conduct, he took psychoanalysis in the direction of consistently focusing on the patient's experience and its meaning (Kohut, 1958). This methodological turn must now be extended to the collection of developmental data. It may then become possible to construct a paradigm of development consistent with self psychology.

The concept of "meaning" is most difficult to define. Since it is central to my discussion I will give a brief if incomplete definition of the way in which I will be using it. We use language to communicate with others. Language, whether verbal or nonverbal, is made up of a set of signs. These signs can include both cognitive and affective dimensions of discourse. Meanings are attached to linguistic signs, such as words, pictures, gestures, musical sounds, and so on. The signs within a language do not mirror the events with which we tend to associate them, rather they are interpretations that mediate the events or perceptions and the meanings attached to them. In the psychoanalytic literature the concept of "representation" is often used to refer to the meanings attached to experiences. This concept is fraught with difficulties however and is the subject of much controversy. I will therefore avoid its use, although much of the time the meaning generally associated with that concept will be the same as that I attach to the construct "the meaning of experience." Meanings, then, are the residues incorporated within the linguistic signs we use. They are the translations we make of occurrences to which we are exposed. They are the currency we use to dialogue with others in our community.

I now turn to a brief discussion of the terms "paradigm," "narrative," and "root metaphor" as necessary introduction to my substantive discussion.

Paradigms: The term "paradigm" was popularized by Kuhn in his classic work *The Structure of Scientific Revolutions* (1970a). In that work, Kuhn sought to establish the thesis that in the history of the natural sciences a succession of different theories gained ascendancy. Each theory had a period of hegemony only to find itself overthrown and displaced by a different theory. Theories, which Kuhn called paradigms, consist of sets of propositions or hypotheses that order investigators' observations. The hypotheses are law-like statements that describe causal relationships between events. The laws embodied in these hypotheses are universally applicable irrespective of the context. According to Kuhn, paradigms can never be falsified, since their authors may always amend their theories to make the data fit into them. When a paradigm is overthrown, it is simply replaced by a new one which redefines the terms previously used, giving these terms new meaning, and thus redefining what constitutes data. It is possible to infer from this thesis that theories are no more than culture-bound editions of explanations scientists give of their surroundings. Each edition reflects the bias of a particular period in history. Paradigms are therefore neither verifiable nor falsifiable.

Kuhn was uncomfortable with the inferences drawn from his work, and was roundly criticized for his views (Lakatos & Musgrave, 1970). At the time of the publication of his work, in 1962, most philosophers of science operated from within a positivist philosophical framework. They regarded paradigms as a set of "nomothetic" propositions that represent the laws that govern the workings of the universe. Knowledge, they believed, is reducible to a small set of such scientifically verifiable principles. For these philosophers of science the notion that knowledge was culture bound was unacceptable because it meant that it was relativistic, that is, each culture's set of truths could be challenged by the truths of other cultures. Kuhn responded to his critics by saying that he did not intend to propose such an extreme position. He expressed the belief that it is possible for each successive paradigm to lead to an increase in knowledge that incrementally brings us closer to the truth (Kuhn, 1970b).

In those days, psychoanalysts such as Hartmann (1958,1964) and Rapaport (1951,1960), hoped to emulate the model of the natural sciences and move psychoanalytic theory to the status of a paradigm. They wished to discover the general laws that guide development and the functioning of the mind. According to their view, a developmental theory formulates the universal phases or stages through which children mature. Theories of psychopathology similarly express the universality of neurotic conflict, or could model themselves after the medical view that toxins, such as traumata, are responsible for patients' illnesses. Finally, a model technique for the practice of psychoanalysis could be devised. If followed, this model would lead to the resolution of internal conflict or reverse the effects of prior experiences.

With the decline of positivism, these hopes faded, both for psychoanalysts and for the philosopher of science. Hermeneutic and social constructivism approaches, with their relativistic biases, displaced the certainty that the positivists wished to attain (Berger & Luckmann, 1966; Gergen & Gergen, 1983, 1986; Hoffman, 1992; McGuire, 1990; Ricoeur, 1980). Critics of positivism offered an alternate view. They held that realities are multiple rather than singular and fixed; all data are theory bound and contextual, rather than objective and decontextualized; the observer and the observed cannot be separated; since it is not possible to establish causal relationships between events, only the recognition of patterns in sequences of events is possible; and, finally, inquiry is never entirely value free (Guba, 1990). These precepts led to the conclusion that theories are "ideographic" that is, they provide descriptive metaphors of the phenomena they cover. Each discipline bases itself on different belief systems, different methodologies, and each aspires to different goals. Some radical critics of positivism went as far as to claim that even the natural sciences offer no more than sophisticated narratives of the segment of the universe they explain. Others insisted that there are irreconcilable differences between the natural and the social sciences. They claimed that while positivist approaches are successful for the natural sciences, constructivist or hermeneutic approaches are more appropriate to the social sciences.

In the discussion so far I have simplified the issues by presenting polarized positions. In reality the controversy is very complex with numerous participants presenting differing views in the debate. The point I wish to make is that the trend is to look at the role of language in the formulation of our conceptual schemes as a way out of what appear as unresolvable problems. I will elaborate later on the perspective that semiotics offers in clarifying some of the issues and providing an acceptable resolution.

Narratives: Until recently, the term "narrative" was used to characterize a literary form of written expression. The term was applied to such works as epics, sagas, romances, novels, whodunits, and other genres (Polkinghorne, 1988; Scholes & Kellog, 1966). In October 1979, the Institute for Psychoanalysis co-sponsored with the University of Chicago, a symposium titled "Narrative: The Illusion of Sequence" (Mitchell, 1980). Among the participants in this symposium were Hayden White and Roy Schafer, and the philosophers Jacques Derrida, Nelson Goodman, and Paul Ricoeur. Among the issues they addressed was the question: What do historians add to a simple chronicle of events that transforms the text into a narrative rather than representing an account that corresponds with what truly happened? One of the participants (White, 1980) noted that the difference between a chronicle and a historical account, i.e., a narrative, is that the chronicle provides a simple list of events, while a historical account adds to those events a theme that unifies and gives coherence to the account. The historian is the agent who interprets the chronicle and adds the theme that makes the story intelligible. Robert Scholes, a literary scholar who was a participant in the symposium, was moved to say that " . . narrative . . . is an 'opiate' which mystifies our understanding by providing a false sense of coherence, an 'illusion of sequence' " (Scholes, 1980, p. viii).

In a different context, Scholes and his colleague Kellog, in their work *The Nature of Narrative* (1966), gave two distinguishing characteristics of a narrative: (a) the presence of a story and a storyteller (p. 4), and, (b) it's fictional rather than factual or historical character. Sarbin, a psychologist, extends the application of the concept of narrative beyond the fictional. He argues that the case histories that clinicians write are narrative in character. In contrast to the literary definition of the term he gives the following definition:

> . . . *narrative* is coterminous with *story* as used by ordinary speakers of English. A story is a symbolized account of actions of human beings that has a temporal dimension. The story has a beginning, a middle, and an ending. The story is held together by recognizable patterns of events called plots. Central to the plot structure are human predicaments and attempted resolutions. (Sarbin, 1986; p. 3)

This definition of narrative has become popular in psychotherapeutic circles. The question I pose is whether this definition of narrative is applicable to some of the developmental theories we construct, rather than just to the case histories we write (Polkinghorne, 1988). The position states that developmental theorists do not simply chronicle the events of childhood. Rather, as historians of childhood, they add their own interpretations and thematic organization to those observations. The resulting theory resembles a narrative rather than a paradigm, as narratives they have beginnings, middles and ends, plots or a central dramatic theme, and a protagonist who is the agent of the action (Howard, 1991; Schafer, 1980, 1981, 1983; Spence, 1982, 1987; White, 1980). Advocates of this position maintain that facts are not simple observables or natural units, rather, theory defines what to consider as a fact. Gaps in the theory are filled in by following the narrative thread of the metaphor, extending the metaphor to describe what remains puzzling. Theories, therefore, provide an intellectual framework that serves as a guide to the collection and organization of the data into a unified system (Sherwood, 1969). The broader question I will examine later is whether it is possible to make a distinction between paradigms and narratives.

Root metaphors: Pepper (1942) describes the concept of root metaphor as follows:

> A man desiring to understand the world looks about for a clue to its comprehension. He pitches upon some area of common sense fact and tries to understand other areas in terms of this one. This original idea becomes his basic analogy or root metaphor. He describes as

best he can the characteristics of this area, or . . . discriminates its structure. He undertakes to interpret all fact in terms of these categories. (p. 91)

Theories attempt to redescribe parts of the universe through a metaphor. This metaphor explains the phenomena more meaningfully because, at first, it translates them into a language that is more understandable. As the theory grows in complexity, the theorist introduces a technical language that makes the phenomena more experience distant, and more abstract.

Pepper suggests that an examination of intellectual history reveals that six root metaphors were used to model the universe (Pepper, 1942; Sarbin, 1986). They are animism, formism, mysticism, mechanism, organicism, and contextualism. Of these six, the ones with which we are most familiar in the psychological domain are the mechanistic and the organismic root metaphors. With the arrival of the narrative approach, the contextual metaphor is now gaining in popularity.

Root metaphors lead observers to frame the questions they pose within the language of the metaphor. Consequently, the answers follow from the analogies made to the metaphor. So, for example, if a theory uses the metaphor that the mind is like a computer, then the answer to the question of what constitutes pathology is that a break down of the computer occurred. The conceptual categories applied to the phenomena come from the model used by the metaphor. Since phenomena do not fall into "natural categories" the metaphor dictates the categories that divide the field of observation and hence shapes those observations. Adherence to a root metaphor compels the theorist to maintain the perspective of that metaphor or risk incoherence. If the theorist steps outside the metaphor to account for phenomena, the result is a mixed metaphor. As we know, mixing metaphors is a cardinal sin in literary expression, in the construction of theories it assures conceptual confusion.

We can compare and/or contrast the root metaphors theories use. We can also direct criticisms at a theory for its use of a particular root metaphor. Or, we can maintain that one root metaphor is superior to another if it presents fewer conceptual problems than others. However, it is not possible to argue that one root metaphor gives a more accurate description of the universe than another. Such a statement presumes that the metaphor is not a metaphor for, but a presentation of, reality.

Theories that incorporate the mechanistic and organismic root metaphors acquire a narrative structure by virtue of the narrative thread these metaphors impart to the data. As such, these theories cannot qualify to the status of paradigms.

Contrast and comparisons: There are critical distinctions between paradigms, narratives, and root metaphors as these relate to the structure of developmental theories. For a theory to be a paradigm it must claim to give an accurate description of the universe of phenomena it covers. The criterion for the validity of a paradigm is its correspondence to the domain it describes. It is arguable whether all paradigms use metaphors in the descriptions they give of phenomena, or whether, as some claim, these descriptions mirror reality itself. This complex issue cannot be addressed in this paper. I will maintain that some theories that use metaphors to re-describe the domain the theory encompasses can achieve the status of paradigms while making no claim to "represent," or give a positivistic view of, reality.

Bruner distinguishes between two modes of thought: The paradigmatic and the narrative. He characterizes the paradigmatic or logico-scientific as attempting "to fulfill the ideal of a formal, mathematical system of description and explanation" (Bruner, 1986; p. 12). The logico-scientific deals with causes. The paradigms the natural sciences offer consist of descriptive and explanatory statements of some portion of the universe. They offer a perspective from which technological advances follow. These paradigms are subject to correction (they are made up of hypothesis that may be falsified); they are based on a correspondence theory of knowledge. Narratives, on the other hand, "lead(s) instead to good stories, gripping drama, believable (though not necessarily "true") historical accounts. It deals in human or human-like intention and action and the vicissitudes and consequences that mark their course" (p. 13).

Narratives and paradigms are antithetical in the goals they strive to achieve. Whereas paradigms are composed of propositional statements that shun the sorts of plots common to narrative, integral to any narrative is a specific plot that guides the action in a particular direction. Furthermore, the propositions put forward by paradigms claim universal applicability, while the accounts given by narratives portray the occurrences within a circumscribed domain. When narratives reach for universal applicability they become myths. Myths represent a particular culture's ethos, but they are different from the collection of propositions that are distinctive of a paradigm. To state that all paradigms are narratives not only nullifies this important distinction but also leads to the slippery slope of relativism. By definition, narratives are products of the author's imagination, they are personal and individual interpretations of the occurrences they portray. They are culture-bound products that may be true for a community but have no validity beyond that community. Other communities may offer competing narratives to "explain" the same set of occurrences. The choice of narrative is arbitrary based on criteria set by cultural preferences.

However, the equation of paradigms and narratives makes science, as a generalized human enterprise with an accepted set of hypotheses, impossible.

In summary, I am suggesting that paradigms cannot be narratives, and narratives cannot be paradigms. Each of these is a distinct discourse that serves a different purpose. While both paradigms and narratives share the common usage of metaphorical expressions, the fact that some root metaphors compel a narrative structure onto a theory does not mean that all root metaphors do so. When a root metaphor has such a structure it cannot legitimately be used in the construction of a paradigm.

To illustrate this point, in what follows I discuss some psychoanalytic developmental theories that use mechanistic and organismic root metaphors. I hope to demonstrate that developmental theories that model themselves on these metaphors use thematic plots that impart coherence to the phenomena. These themes are like the "opiate" to which Scholes refers, they give the illusion of sequence and reality, and impart a narrative structure to the theory. I will argue that a theory that relies on a contextual metaphor can avoid these difficulties.

Because of the methodological problems this analysis presents, this paper may itself be regarded as a story, or a narrative, that deals playfully with the issues surrounding the formulation of psychoanalytic developmental theories. My discussion of developmental theories may appear reductionistic, or seem to caricature the positions I am describing. While this may in part be true, I do not believe that I significantly distort the positions I present.

ROOT METAPHORS IN DEVELOPMENTAL THEORIES

Models Based on Mechanistic Principles

The mechanistic metaphor is the dominant metaphor in the physical sciences. The descriptive perspective is the only perspective that is consistent with this metaphor. Phenomena are analogous to the components of a machine. The universe is like a perfect automaton whose laws it is the task of scientists to discover. The modern variants of the mechanistic metaphor compare the mind to a computer that processes information (Holt, 1972).

Freud's Mechanistic/Hydraulic Model

Freud's dynamic point of view is perhaps the best example of a mechanistic/hydraulic model of the functioning of mind (1917, 1924). The mind is like a steam engine that deals with the pressures produced by sexual or aggressive drives. In the structural point of view, the concept of the "ego apparatus" is an example of the mechanistic model of psychic functioning (1923). The ego, in the structural point of view, is an energy processing apparatus that transforms primitive, unneutralized, primary process energy into more refined, usable and sublimated secondary process energy. The filtering system that effects this transformation is the ego that moves the energy from the id to the object that it cathects and back to the ego. Ego development occurs through the vicissitudes of attachment to, and loss of, objects. Without the outward flow of energy, the system clogs up as the energy becomes trapped in the system itself. When that occurs, the result is psychopathology in the form of regressions or arrests that lead to narcissistic, or other disorders.

As is readily evident, this metaphor approaches psychological phenomena descriptively. It presumes that it is possible to infer the mechanisms that operate in the mind from the behaviors, thoughts, fantasies, and dreams a person presents. In its developmental theory, this metaphor redescribes the common phenomena of attachment. It retranslates them into the figure of speech the metaphor dictates. And, it extends the analogy to explain failures in the developmental progression.

The Information Processing Theory of Basch

The choice of information processing theory, as a root metaphor, was influenced by the advances in communications theory, systems theory, cybernetics, and artificial intelligence. These advances led to the notion that the best model to help understand the workings of the mind is the computer. It is, therefore, possible to categorize this approach to development as using a mechanistic metaphor since it uses a computer model of the mind (Daehler & Bukatko, 1985; Gardner, 1985).

The communications model assumes that two basic principles operate during growth: The principle of entropy, and the principle of increasing complexity within a hierarchical organization. As stated in the second law of thermodynamics (the principle of entropy) the movement of the universe is in the direction of increasing disorganization, or chaos. While there are islands in which greater organization arises periodically, the direction of the system is toward a steady state in which the existing energy will be evenly dispersed throughout the universe. Organization eventually will cease to exist. Messages passed along, as in the parlor game of "telephone," deteriorate to the point where the original message is no longer recognizable from the last form of its expression. Yet paradoxically, islands of impressive organization appear: babies are born, books are written, speeches made, and institutions appear. All of these appear to move the system in a different direction, in seeming defiance of entropy. In fact, before being washed away by the waves of time, the growth that occurs through the production of these complex hierarchies of structures are the product of the information encoded in the system. Similarly, the brain encodes information through a set of programs that are transmitted genetically. The genes encapsulate a set of algorithms that determine the structure and function of each element within the organism.

In recent years Basch (1976, 1988) has been a strong and articulate advocate of this position. It is his conviction that as an explanatory theory it represents the best effort to complete the project that Freud began but left unfinished. According to Basch the reason Freud was forced to give up the project was because the state of knowledge regarding neurological function was not sufficiently advanced to provide answers to the problems he was attempting to solve.

Basch gives up the concept of mind altogether. For him this concept bears a historical relationship to the totally unscientific concept of the soul, for the mind is nothing more than brain function. One can substitute a description of cortical and subcortical function for explanations currently couched in the language of mental processes. Pattern matching is the fundamental mechanism that allows the brain to order information. "What computers and the brain–indeed, all living cells–have in common is that their output or behavior is determined by the information generated from the input: therefore, the analogy between the pattern matching of the computer and the brain" (Basch, 1988, p. 52).

Basch conceives of a developmental spiral as characterizing the developmental progression. The struggle to achieve competence is central to every person's functioning. "Pattern matching is the neurological counterpart of the experience of competence, the brain functions like an analogue computer" (p. 53). Competence leads to self-esteem that in turn allows the person to make decisions expressed through behavior. The affects provide the motives for thought and behavior.

For Basch the self is a system that reflects the affective and cognitive information-processing activities of the brain. Psychopathology results from the unsatisfactory compromises the self system makes during adaptation. This is not a comprehensive developmental theory but the outline of what might evolve into a theory. On the other hand, I should mention that Basch is quite complimentary of Stern's model of the development of the sense of self in infants and may find it compatible with his framework.

Models Based on Organismic Principles

The organismic metaphor is grounded on biological principles. In psychology the analogy is drawn between the mind and organisms that require nourishment to grow. Organisms have their own timetable of phases or stages. The observational perspectives suitable for this metaphor are the descriptive and the interpersonal.

The organismic root metaphor is the most popular metaphor in psychological circles. Developmental theorists who favor this metaphor conceive of the human mind as an organism that becomes progressively differentiated from less developed (i.e., immature) to more developed (i.e., mature) states. As an organism, the mind requires nutriment to develop and grow. The nutriment comes in the form of an exchange between the partners in a relationship. The child forms an attachment to a caregiver and takes nourishment in the form of love, care, affection, devotion, or atunement. Children ingest the nutriments through processes such as imitation, internalization, and identification. They metabolize what they ingest which turns it into psychic structure.

Other psycho-biological processes include the principles of: homeostasis, of flight/fight response to danger, or of adaptation. Normality is measurable either by the extent to which the person approximates an ideal state of growth and maturation, or by the extent to which the person adapts to his or her environment. On the other hand, since the person's psychic unfolding is dependent on nutriment provided by caregivers, failure to receive appropriate nourishment and exposure to toxins, that is, to traumata, leads to psychopathology.

In what follows I summarize three organismic models to illustrate this perspective: the ingestion model of Freud (1912, 1917; Schafer, 1968), the embryological model of Mahler (1968, 1975), and the translocation model of Kohut (1971, 1977, 1984).

The Ingestion Model: Freud: Internalization

As stated earlier, the ingestion model postulates that during development an exchange occurs between child and caregiver in which the child is the recipient of something the caregiver provides. The "something" given takes the form of psychic nutriment. For example, Freud proposed the view that the child invests the object with libidinal energy. Following its investment of an object the child incorporates the object in the "oral mode." The nutriment is the relationship the object provides to further the child's cathexis of the caregiver. That is, the nutritional value of the attachment becomes protein for the growing child. The child ingests and metabolizes what the caregiver provides. As a result, psychic structure and ego growth occur. The ego thus becomes the repository of lost objects with whom the person has identified or ingested. The theory depicts the child as a passively expectant recipient and/or as an active consumer of what the object offers (Schafer, 1968).

This model emphasizes the adequacy, or inadequacy, of the attachment to the object. It values the object's responsiveness to the needs of the child, seeing it as determining whether the child will progress successfully through the subsequent developmental phases. If the nutriment the object offers is toxic, i.e., wrapped in anger or detachment, then the child develops a case of psychic indigestion, and cannot metabolize the incorporated object. Kernberg (1975, 1976) follows M. Klein (1950, 1955), who plays many variations on this theme as she describes the vicissitudes of children's psychic indigestion. The child may throw up what he or she has taken in, as in the paranoid position. Or, the child may re-ingest what he or she has thrown up, as in projective identification. Or, the child may refuse further nourishment, collapse into an anorectic, depressed state, as in the depressive position, and fail to thrive.

The Embryological Model: Mahler: Differentiation

In Mahler's model the infant is born in a state of non-differentiation and grows from a symbiotic state, to achieve separateness and individuation. In this organismic model the child is bio-genetically preprogrammed to move through the various phases of its organization, much like the processes that occur in cell division. Psychological birth, and the processes of separation and individuation, are analogous to the division of a fertilized egg as embryologists describe it. The mother's psyche represents the initial fertilized egg. The infant's psyche is at first totally undifferentiated from that of the mother. As the nucleus of a self forms in the infant, a state of symbiosis occurs. Slowly a membrane begins to form around the nucleus. This process launches the process of separation. Ultimately when the infant has its own membrane, and also its own well-formed nucleus, the process is completed. Cell division occurs at the end of the separation-individual phase with the establishment of object constancy. Object constancy is an indicator that the structures laid down are complete. For Mahler, growth reflects the formation of a self and an object representation. These representations result from the internalization of aspects of the person(s) with whom the child formed an attachment. Since this model also accepts the principles of the ingestion model, even the unconscious contents of the mother's psychic structure are transferable to the child. The characteristic patterns of mutual influence in the purely social exchanges between mother and infant provide an important basis for structuring the infant's experience. Representations of the self, the other, and the relationship all evolve simultaneously. They are inextricably linked together.

Here again, the child moves along the developmental progression unless interferences occur. These interferences may stem either from faulty bio-genetic programming—as with autistic children—or, from insufficient nourishment—as in borderline children, for whom the environment did not provide adequate responses during the rapproachment sub-phase of development.

The Translocation Model: Kohut: Transmuting Internalization

To the extent that Kohut adopted a modified version of the ingestion model his theory is inconsistent with his stated purpose of purifying psychoanalysis of biological elements (Kohut, 1958). For him selfobjects provide an essential ingredient in the growth process. Kohut called the process "transmuting internalization." In an early paper on this concept Tolpin (1978) describes the slow bit-by-bit acquisition of selfobject functions. The caregiver complements the child's sense of self by providing selfobject functions. Then, through optimal frustration the caregivers allow the child to begin to exercise his/her capacities unaware, at first, of the absence of the caregiver. When optimal disillusionment with the idealized object occurs, the capacity is transferred and resides in the child. While no person becomes totally freed of the need for others—we all need ongoing nourishment to survive—a qualitative change occurs that denotes the internalization of some of these functions. The result is that the person no longer continues to need the archaic form of the function or nourishment, but acquires the capacity for a more mature version of the selfobject function.

Atwood and Stolorow (1984) have aptly termed this form of growth as a process through which "selfobjects are translocated" (p. 39). Although the type of ingestion Kohut proposes is different from that of the libidinal model, the person ingests the *functions of the object* rather than *parts of the object*; nevertheless, by retaining the concept of optimal frustration he reintroduces the organismic metaphor. Since Kohut rejected drive theory, his retention of this process leads to difficulties which some of his followers have tried to correct by substituting the concept of optimal responsiveness. However, one is left with the impression that the caregivers must titrate the amount of nourishment they provide to the child for it to be digestible. These inconsistencies in self psychology make it difficult to articulate an experience near developmental theory that avoids the organismic metaphor, which reifies psychological processes, and retains a focus on the meaning of experience to the patient.

Psychoanalytic Developmental Theories–Narratives or Paradigms?

In looking over the metaphors these developmental theorists use, it is difficult to escape the conclusion that the theories present a set of narratives to explain the phenomena. Freud's use of the mechanistic metaphor attributes to an agent–the drives–the capacity to propel development in a particular direction. This agent is pre-programmed to achieve two goals: the discharge of excess energy and the retention of a homeostatic balance. The plot in this narrative is generated by the conflict between the forces that seek to discharge energy and those that prevent its discharge. Basch's metaphor conceals the agent in the mechanism that functions to match the patterns of incoming stimuli with those existing in the brain. The plot is more subtle in that it consists of a hierarchy of algorithms that encode the patterns and that generate responses. These algorithms are themselves fueled by the affects.

In the case of the organismic metaphor, an agent also guides the action, usually called an ego or a self. This agent goes through stages or phases that identify life span issues. We can speak of this life-span as having a beginning, middle, and end. The agent is engaged in a dramatic struggle to achieve maturity. This struggle may revolve around whether the person will attain object constancy, reach separation/individuation, resolve the Oedipus, adapt to the environment, or maintain self-cohesion (Holt, 1972; Schafer, 1980, 1981). These metaphors reify the processes through which growth occurs.

Also contributing to the narrative structure of these theories are the observational methods used by investigators. Historically, investigators of children's development have used one of two perspectives to collect data. Each of these perspectives places the observer in a spatial location in relation to the observed; he or she becomes a spectator of the process rather than an interpreter of the meanings of events to the child. These descriptive perspectives place observers outside the phenomena; the subjective perspective places the observer within the person, while the interpersonal or intersubjective, places the observers at the interface between the observer and the observed. The interpersonal presumes the observer to be located outside the interaction, while the intersubjective places the observer within the interaction. Observers who take the descriptive perspective take "God's eye view" or what Nagel (1986) called "the view from nowhere." They claim to give an objective account of the phenomena from a neutral position. They may or may not assume the independent existence of a universe that is unaffected by their activities. If they assume its independent existence, they claim to discover facts; if they do not, they believe themselves to construct events from their cultural context. In any case, the observers become "objective" narrators–story tellers–of the unfolding development of the child.

I want to emphasize that advocates of these positions reify psychological processes. But understanding human conduct is not only the disclosure of observed phenomena, whether external or internal to the person. An essential component of all psychoanalytic understanding is an understanding of the subjective dimension which can only occur when we include the meaning each person attaches to the accompanying events within the context in which these occur (Kohut, 1958; Mishler, 1979). Empathy involves understanding the patient's experience and understanding its meaning to the patient. This dimension is a necessary condition for any psychoanalytic explanation of development. Understanding the meaning of experience involves an interpretive process that elicits the uniqueness of the experience. It is impossible to escape the conclusion that when investigators do not include the domain of meaning in their observations they violate Kohut's injunction that any description of psychological phenomena devoid of an empathic understanding of its meaning to the person is not truly psychoanalytic.

Is a Paradigm of Development Possible?

Several issues converge at this point; among them is the central question of the sense in which a paradigm of development is not a narrative. A discussion of this question must deal with the relationship between a developmental theory and its application to particular cases; it must address the issue of the differences between a historical and a fictitious account; and, finally, it must clarify the reasons for maintaining that the contextual root metaphor is the appropriate metaphor for a developmental paradigm. Once these issues are addressed, it is then possible to resolve the question of the status of developmental theories as paradigms, and clarify the nature of the bridge between developmental theories and clinical theories.

On theories and case histories: It is important to underscore the distinction between paradigms as narratives and the narratives that result from the application of a paradigm to a set of data. I believe that the failure to make this distinction leads to confusion regarding the status of some theories. For example, Schafer claims that, as an analyst, he engages in the co-construction of a narrative with his patients. The fact that the products of his analyses are narratives does not mean that the methods he uses to achieve that end have narrative structure (Schafer, 1992). As Schafer correctly points out in his critique, Freud's metapsychology is itself a narrative or, as Freud himself acknowledged, a myth. While Freud understood this "myth" to be a set of hypotheses within the scientific psychology he proposed, in contrast to other scientific hypotheses, his metapsychology turned out to not be falsifiable as other scientific hypotheses can be. But both Freud's metapsychology and Schafer's method lead to the construction of case histories that are themselves narratives. The distinction is between an explanatory method that has a narrative structure and one that does not. For example, libidinal theory proposes an oedipal phase of development. This theory is a story that generates case histories as stories. In contrast, a theory of trauma that specifies that any event having specific characteristics produces a specified effect on most or all people affected by it offers a "general law" of the traumatic effect of certain events. It does not have a narrative structure, although its application to individual cases most certainly would produce a narrative. Such a theory of trauma could be part of a larger paradigm.

I believe that the failure to make this distinction leads to the confusion that currently exists regarding narrative theory in constructivist circles. For example, Stern's proposal in his paper on "the representation of relational patterns" (1988, 1989) is a theory that explains how children enter into the domain of the narrative self. That is, it explains the domain in which children begin to create narratives about their lives. The theory is not a narrative, its aim is to explain the emergence of life narratives during a phase of childhood. It permits clinicians to understand, and perhaps assist in the construction of, patients' life narratives. The attribution of a narrative structure to the theory is generally related to the confusion between the paradigm and its specific application to a set of data.

The analogy between the grammar of a language and its articulation within a specific linguistic expression best exemplifies the relationship between a theory and its application. Grammars do not provide prototypic sentences that exemplify correct structures (Goldberg, 1995; Makari & Shapiro, 1993). They set out rules by which any sentence can be judged to be well formed or ungrammatical. Similarly, developmental paradigms spell out the processes through which children mature. They elucidate the processes through which changes occur.

Developmental theories that do not begin with a set of hypotheses, but rather proclaim their editions of development to be the only correct ones, present an "ideal type" or "normative" case to which actual cases must conform. They invariably introduce a narrative thread to give coherence to their account. They do so at the expense of finding correspondences between the patient's productions and the actual occurrences. They become prescriptive rather than descriptive. They dictate the course of nature, rather than taking note of its regularities. For reasons that cannot be discussed here, this conclusion argues against the constructivist position that developmental theories are culture-bound products (Cushman, 1991; Saari,1986a, 1986b, 1988, 1991; Saleeby, 1994).

Narrative truth and historical truth. Spence's work (1982, 1987, 1990) raises the important question of how it is possible to distinguish between a patient's historically accurate account from one that is fictitious. In his earlier work (1982) his answer was that it is not possible, although he wished it were possible. It was his belief that we can only rely on the internal coherence of the account to feel satisfied with the outcome of an analysis. This answer raises the fundamental issue of the criterion to use in the search for truth, presuming that as therapists it is truth with which we are concerned.

Philosophers in recent years propose two criteria through which truth may be attained: The criterion of the internal coherence of an account, and the criterion of the correspondence of the account with factual events. The former relies on the sense made of the account; the internal validity of what is offered has priority over the match between patients' recollections and the actual events. For example, therapists who rely on the coherence criterion may decide that a patient must have been sexually abused because that is the only hypothesis that makes sense of the patient's material and the transference. The weakness of this position is that since such a hypothesis cannot be verified for its correspondence with the historical events, there is no way to be assured of its truthfulness. There is no way to distinguish fact from fiction. The latter criterion, that of correspondence, relies on matching recollections with actual events. However, for a clinician to obtain such verification would entail going to sources external to the treatment setting. Clinicians who rely on the sanctity of the transference and the major therapeutic agent are forsworn from using such data or methods of data collection. They face a different, but no less difficult, dilemma than that faced by those who subscribe to the coherence criterion in establishing the truthfulness of a patient's recollections.

Some clinicians claim that their central task is therapeutic rather than investigative. They try to avoid these dilemmas by defining their activities as not concerned with the truth or falsity of their patients' recollections. By taking this position clinicians deprive themselves of any rationale for a theory of developmental psychopathology. They simply have no basis for claiming that past events affect the patient in the here and now, and that the

occurrences within the treatment are related to developmental occurrences.

Cavell (1993), a philosopher who received analytic training, proposes a
way out of this dilemma without sacrificing the need for coherence or
dispensing with the correspondence criterion. She presents a philosophical
position that subscribes to both criteria simultaneously. She states:

> . . . interpretation must marry coherence and correspondence. Neither
> by itself is a sufficient constraint on meaning, nor an adequate crite-
> rion of truth. Let me briefly summarize the argument.
>
> Coherence comes into interpretation this way: describing some-
> one's action . . . imputes to him certain beliefs and desires; it tells us
> something about how he sees the world, or "under what descrip-
> tion." And the content of any one belief or desire, any one descrip-
> tion, is a function of its place in a network of others.
>
> But correspondences comes in as well; for in our encounter with
> someone we want to understand, we must be able to find a relation
> between his words and what we can see going on in our common
> world. If we cannot at some point tie words to a shared material
> reality, understanding can't get started. (p. 87)

In order to understand more fully this position, it is necessary to step
back and consider the role of language and meaning in the construction of
any conceptual framework. Language is a system of signs that we, as sign
users, share with a community of others with whom we communicate.
These signs encode a set of meanings which derive from the context in
which the sign user is embedded. The signs of a language are cultural
products which, to an extent, are arbitrary symbols for referents (denota-
tive and/or connotative) in the world. Each culture generates its own set of
signs, each has its own set of arbitrary referents representing the way in
which that culture divides its perceptual and conceptual world.

Constructivists tend to emphasize this arbitrary dimension of signs in
languages to argue that all cultures construct their realities, that knowledge
is relative to the cultural context, and that the culture's values permeate the
language used by the group. For them, communication is possible only
because the meanings attached to a particular language (sign system) are
shared by the sign users. Shared meanings result from the negotiations that
occur between sign users. Some interpret this position to imply that since
the concepts of each language are embedded in that culture's world view, it
is impossible to translate those concepts into a different language (cf., the
"Whorf-Sapir hypothesis" in Gardner, 1972; p. 181). Cited in support of
this view is the worn-out example that because of the number of meanings

of the concept of "snow" in the Eskimo vocabulary it is untranslatable into any other language. The meaning of a concept changes as a word from a different language is used. The argument is also made that a culture's developmental theory is no more that a narrative constructed by the culture to describe what is normative for that culture. Thus, Cushman (1991) claims that Stern's use of the concept of "self" is a culture-bound product of the Western notion that people are units that embody selves. Since this notion is not possessed by all cultures, Stern's developmental scheme does not have universal validity. Gergen (1985), in a similar constructivist position, claims that all psychological concepts are culture bound and derive from an "essentialist" perspective. This is a perspective that maintains that the concept refers to qualities that reside within people. For example, for Gergen, anger is a form of social role which, as a term, does not refer to mental states, but is part of the role itself. He states: "The explanatory locus of human action shifts from the interior region of the mind to the processes and structure of human interaction" (p. 271). The implication, again, is that no general developmental theory can exist, since such a theory would have to posit universal "essences" which people possess. Any explanation of development that hopes to include the effect of endowment, genetic givens or deficits, becomes infeasible according to this position. Constructivists, therefore, reject the correspondence theory of knowledge, and hew to the coherence view of knowledge.

A different view of language is that presented by the philosopher C.S. Peirce (Buchler, 1955; Houser & Kloesel, 1992). He defines a sign as "something which stands to somebody for something in some respect or capacity" (Buchler, p. 99). He suggests that there are three components to signs: They may be pictures, gestures, or words. The sign stands for an object which may be an actual physical entity, a concept, or the figment of one's imagination. The sign and its object are brought into relationship to one another by someone, i.e., a person, whom Peirce designates as "an interpretant." The interpretant stands for the embodied capacity to decode what signs stand for in relation to their objects. The significance of Peirce's proposal is that it anchors language–as a system of signs–into a context without which it cannot exist. The context is the actual world of which human beings are a part. This context represents what we generally call "external reality." It is the object to which we refer through the use of language. Language is inseparable from its interpretants, and, the objects to which language refers are independent, continuous, and unyielding to the interpretants' wishes that they be different.

The implication of this semiotic perspective for theories of development is that as human beings we share a common set of experiences by virtue of our participation in a common cultural heritage and language. These experiences are interpreted by us and encoded into a set of signs. All the referents to these signs, however, are not our creations. We do not construct our realities, even though our language may color our realities. There are universal attributes from which we cannot detach. For example, facial expression reflects a set of basic affects which are the same across many cultures. The names attached to those affects differ from culture to culture, but the basic feelings have universal common meanings. Based on this we can hypothesize a correspondence between the triggering events, the experiences, and the resulting feelings as reflected in the facial expression. A developmental paradigm that articulates generalities that have universal significance becomes possible.

As Cavell points out, we share a language that provides a set of shared meanings. These meanings derive from experiences in the real world with which they bear some correspondence. Through our language we are caught in a web of meanings that pervades all our relationships. This web is not disconnected from the world, rather it is tethered to it by the language we share.

The constraints imposed by the correspondence of the events to the occurrences to which they refer distinguish a historical account from a fictitious account. We may call these constraints "invariants" which are inviolable if we are to claim a correspondence between the history and the events the history describes. Among these invariants are the following: (a) the time frame in which the action occurred must be fixed and cannot be violated; (b) the characters who were participants in the actions must remain identical; (c) the sequence in which the events occurred must remain constant; and finally, (d) the setting of the action cannot be modified. Changes in any of these invariants produces a historically inaccurate and hence an untruthful account of what occurred. Beyond these invariants is the common language speakers use to refer to these events and communicate with each other. If we cannot, in good faith, believe that each of us refers to common events from shared experiences then we are left in an Alice in Wonderland world in which words mean what each wishes them to mean, and communication is impossible. In works of fiction these constraints do not exist. The author's imagination is free to rearrange time sequences, participants, settings, in any way that suits his or her plot, as in the movie *Back to the Future*, where the entertainment value lies in the novel rearrangement of the sequence in which the events took place. Therapists, as historians, have no such freedom in the reconstruction of their patients' pasts.

Added to these constraints is the human need to impose coherence upon our experiences. What is subject to interpretation in any historical account, and hence adds narrative color and coherence to it, is the plot that surrounds the relationships between these invariants. That is, the factors that influence the protagonist, the protagonist's motives or intentions, the personal meanings the events have to the story teller, the relationships between the people involved in the action, and other participants in the action. These latter factors are tied together through the coherence of the account.

Cavell's point then is that our shared language gives access to both subjective states and presumed objective facts. It thus avoids the dilemma of the bifurcation of historical and narrative truths. Language, verbal and nonverbal, is grounded in a set of meanings that are tied to the world in ways that we take for granted. A paradigm of development grounded on the meanings people derive from their experiences becomes possible. The danger that the hypotheses in such a paradigm would be totally culturally derived is avoided by virtue of the fact that concepts are grounded in the experiences from which they are drawn. They are subject to verification and falsification across cultural domains. This conclusion leads to a consideration of the contextual metaphor as the more appropriate metaphor for such a paradigm.

The contextual metaphor: The contextual metaphor avoids some of the objectionable aspects of the mechanistic and ingestion models of growth. Pepper (1942) states:

> When we come to contextualism, we pass from an analytical into a synthetic type of theory. It is characteristic of the synthetic theories that their root metaphors cannot satisfactorily be denoted even to first approximation by well-known common-sense concepts . . . The best term out of common sense to suggest the point of origin of contextualism is probably the historic event." (p. 232)

The contextual metaphor is drawn from the pragmatic philosophers who subscribe to a world view in which systems are wholes that cannot be understood as mere agglomerations of parts. Each system is composed of a set of interrelated elements whose sum is greater that the sum of the individual parts. Furthermore, any part cannot be understood independently of other parts, though not every part is necessarily relatable to every other part.

I propose that it is possible to construct a developmental theory using this metaphor by focusing on the domain of meaning. Such a theory would be very different from the traditional developmental theories discussed above. Its aim would be to give an account of the genesis and organization of the meanings of experience. Its task is to examine human experience and its encoding into a set of signs. It will explain how a person construes meanings from self-experience, and give an account of the elements that shape the meanings of those experiences; it will clarify the way in which each person develops a unique interpretation of the particular life episodes to which he or she is exposed, and describe the progression through which each person moves to gather the components of self-experience into meaningful themes that integrate the parts into a whole. This whole will then constitute the person's self-narrative.

Among the compelling reasons, therefore, for turning to the contextual metaphor for assistance in the construction of developmental theories are the following: It is consistent with an observational perspective that gives primacy to the meaning of experience, it is congruent with the notion of a language system that provides a set of signs through which meanings are shared, and it gives promise of providing an explanatory theory for the structuring of narratives.

CONCLUSION

If part of the function of a developmental theory is to provide clinicians with the means with which to identify the sources of a patient's problems, then a relationship must be established between the present-day problems and their historical emergence. If that cannot be done, the developmental theory becomes superfluous. The bridge between a developmental theory and the occurrences in the clinical setting is a theory of psychopathology. Reliance on a coherence criterion alone to knit together the narrative a patient presents precludes the need for such a bridge, and undermines the principles of a developmental psychopathology. If there is no way to establish that actual sexual abuse occurred, how can we be assured that the symptoms a patient manifests are the result of sexual abuse? Without knowledge of a cause we cannot claim to know that the effect was produced by that cause. But since we are precluded from gathering evidence as in a court of law from other sources, we must rely on the knowledge that in ordinary discourse our language is shared by others in our context and also grounded in common experiences.

In the clinical setting, patients through their discourse refer to events in the real world. We distinguish neurosis from psychosis not only by virtue of the incoherence of a psychotic's discourse, and not because this discourse is not part of a shared set of meanings that are untranslatable, but also because the referents of the communications appear to us not substantiated in reality. While these issues raise complex questions regarding the authority of the therapist to judge what is real and what is not, these problems are not insurmountable. They deserve detailed discussion that must be deferred to a future time.

A psychoanalytic developmental theory consistent with self psychology is one that seeks to understand the development of the child's subjectivity. It addresses the ways in which children become language users, and how they are socialized into a community's modes of communication. Most of all it presents a hypothetical scheme for the processes that contribute to the emergence and organization of the meanings of self-experience. Such a theory could gain the status of a paradigm.

If the sense of self is not the product of the ingestion of experiences of interactions with others, or the translocation of the psychic contents and functions of others, and if it is not the result of inputs of varied experiences processed through algorithms of increasing complexity, how are we to think of the sense of self? I suggest that what it means to be a self is best understood as the process through which the meanings of experiences are disclosed to and acquired by people, and through the set of activities through which people integrate those experiences into a coherent set of meanings that constitute their self-narrative.

To be a self is to be a member of a community of sign users (Palombo, 1992). Subjectivity, language acquisition and usage go hand in hand. Shared meanings anchor each person within reality, not simply because that reality is constructed by the community in which the person is raised, but because the language is reflective of something beyond itself which others experience as well. Understanding or describing development entails giving an account of the processes through which the world takes shape for the child. A self apart from a community of others which provides the context for the emergence of meaningful exchanges is meaningless. The dialogue between child and caregiver is the playing field in which the child's sense of self and that of the caregiver interact. Empathy is the means through which much of this dialogue is conducted.

BIBLIOGRAPHY

Atwood, G. E. & Stolorow, R. D. (1984), *Structures of subjectivity: Explorations in psychoanalytic phenomenology.* New York: The Analytic Press.

Basch, M. F. (1976), Psychoanalysis and Communication Science. *The Annual of Psychoanalysis*, Vol. 4. New York: Universities Press. Pp. 385-421.

Basch, M. F. (1988), *Understanding Psychotherapy: The Science Behind The Art.* New York: Basic Books.

Berger, P. L. & Luckmann, T. (1966), *The Social Construction of Reality: A treatise in the sociology of knowledge.* New York: Doubleday, Anchor Books.

Bruner, J. (1986), *Actual Minds and Possible Worlds.* Cambridge: Harvard University Press.

Buchler, J. (Ed.), (1955), *Philosophical Writings of Peirce.* New York: Dover Publications.

Cavell, M. (1993), *The Psychoanalytic Mind: From Freud to Philosophy.* Cambridge: Harvard University Press.

Cushman, P. (1991) Ideology obscured: Political uses of the self in Daniel Stern's infant. *American Psychologist* 46(3)206-219.

Daehler, M. W. & Bukatko, D. (1985), *Cognitive Development.* New York: Alfred A. Knopf.

Freud, S. (1912), *Totem and Taboo.* Standard Edition. Vol. 13. Pp. 1-163.

Freud, S. (1917), *Mourning and Melancholia.* Standard Edition. Vol 14. Pp. 237-242.

Freud, S. (1924), *The dissolution of the Oedipus complex.* Standard Edition, Vol 19. Pp. 173-182.

Freud, S. (1923), *The ego and the id.* Standard Edition, Vol 19. Pp. 3-66.

Gardner, H. (1972), *The Quest for Mind.* Chicago: The University of Chicago Press.

Gardner, H. (1985), *The mind's new science: A history of the cognitive revolution.* New York: Basic Books.

Gergen, K.J. (1985), The social constructionist movement in modern psychology. *American Psychologist* 40(3)266-275.

Gergen, K. J. & Gergen, M. M. (1983), Narratives of the self. From: *Studies In Social Identity.* Sarben T., and Scheibe, K. (Eds.) New York: Praeger. Pp. 254-173.

Gergen, K. J. & Gergen, M. M. (1986), Narrative Form and the construction of psychological science. In Sarbin, T., (Ed.) New York: Praeger. Pp. 22-44.

Goldberg, A., (1995), *The Problem of Perversion.* New Haven: Yale University Press.

Guba, E.G. (1990), The Alternative Paradigm Dialogue. In E.G. Guba (Ed.) *The Paradigm Dialogue.* Newbury Park: Sage Publications. Pp. 17-30.

Hartmann, H. (1958), *Ego psychology and the problem of adaptation.* New York: International Universities Press.

Hartmann, H. (1964), The development of the ego concept in Freud's work. Hartmann, H. *Essays in ego psychology.* New York: International universities Press. Ch 14.

Hoffman, I. Z. (1992), Some Practical Implications Of A Social-Constructivist View Of The Psychoanalytic Situation. *Psychoanalytic Dialogues,* 2(3):287-304.

Holt, R.R. (1972), Freud's mechanistic and humanistic images of man. *Psychoanalysis and Contemporary Science,* 1:3-24.

Houser, N. & Kloesel, C. (Eds.), (1992), *The essential Peirce: Selected philosophical writings.* Vol. I (1867-1893). Bloomington: Indiana University Press.

Howard, G. S. (1991), Culture Tales: A Narrative Approach To Thinking, Cross-Cultural Psychology, And Psychotherapy. *Am Psychologist,* 46(3)187-197.

Kernberg, O.F. (1975), Borderline Conditions and Pathological Narcissism. New York: Jason Aronson.

Kernberg, O.F. (1976), Object relations theory and clinical psychoanalysis. New York: Jason Aronson.

Klein, G. S. (1973), Two theories or one? *Bull Menninger Clinic*, 37:99-132.

Klein, M. (1950), The importance of symbol formation in the development of the ego, 1030. In *Contributions to Psycho-Analysis: 1921-1945*.

Klein, M. (1955), *The psychoanalytic play technique its history and significance. New directions in psychoanalysis. New York: Basic Books.*

Kohut, H. (1959). Introspection, empathy, and psychoanalysis, *Journal of the American Psychoanalytic Association*, 7: 459-483.

Kohut, H. (1971), *The Analysis of the Self.* New York: International Universities Press.

Kohut, H. (1977), *The restoration of the self.* New York: International Universities Press.

Kohut, H. (1984), *How does analysis cure?* Goldberg (Ed). Chicago: The University of Chicago Press.

Kuhn, T. S. (1970a), *The structure of scientific revolutions. Second Edition.* Foundations of the Unity of Science, 2. Chicago: University of Chicago Press.

Kuhn, T, S. (1970b), Reflections on my Critics. In Lakatos, I. & Musgrave, A. (Eds.), (1970), *Criticism and the Growth of Knowledge.* Proceedings of the International Colloquium in the Philosophy of Science, London, 1965, Volume 4. Cambridge: Cambridge University Press. Pp. 231-278.

Lakatos, I. & Musgrave, A. (Eds.) (1970), *Criticism and the Growth of Knowledge.* Proceedings of the International Colloquium in the Philosophy of Science, London, 1965, Volume 4. Cambridge: Cambridge University Press.

Mahler, M. S. (1968), *On human symbiosis and the vicissitudes of individuation.* New York: International Universities Press. Ch 1 & 2.

Mahler et al. (1975), *The psychological birth of the human infant.* New York: Basic Books. Pt II, pp. 39-122.

Makari, G. & Shapiro, T. (1993), On psychoanalytic listening: Language and unconscious communication. *Jour Am Psychoanalytic Assoc*, 41(4):991-1020.

McGuire, M. (1990), The Rhetoric Of Narrative: A Hermeneutic Critical Theory. In: Britton, B. K. & Pellegrini, A. D. (Eds.) *Narrative Thought and Narrative Language.* Hillsdale, N. J.: Lawrence Erlbaum. Pp. 219-236.

Mishler, E. G. (1979), Meaning In Context: Is There Any Other Kind? *Harvard Educational Review*, 49(1):1-19.

Mitchell, W. J. T. (Ed.), (1980), *On Narrative.* Chicago: The University Of Chicago Press.

Nagel, T. (1986), *The View from Nowhere.* Oxford: Oxford University Press.

Palombo, J. (1991a), Bridging The Chasm Between Developmental Theory And Clinical Theory. Part I. The Chasm. In: Goldberg, A. (Ed.) *The Annual of Psychoanalysis Vol XIX*, Hillsdale, N.J.: The Analytic Press. Pp. 151-174.

Palombo, J. (1991b), Bridging The Chasm Between Developmental Theory And Clinical Theory. Part II. The Bridge. In: Goldberg, A. (Ed.) *The Annual of Psychoanalysis Vol XIX*, Hillsdale, N.J.: The Analytic Press. Pp. 175-193.

Palombo, J. (1992), Narratives, Self-Cohesion, And The Patient's Search For Meaning. *Clinical Social Work Jour,* 20(3):249-270.

Pepper, S. (1942), *World Hypotheses.* Berkeley: University of California Press.

Polkinghorne, D. E. (1988), *Narrative Knowing and the Human Sciences.* New York: State University of New York Press.

Rapaport, D. (1951), The conceptual model of psychoanalysis. Gill, M. (Ed.) T*he collected papers of David Rapaport.* New York: Basic Books. Pp. 405-431.

Rapaport, D. (1960), The structure of psychanalytic theory: a systematizing attempt. *Psychological Issue,* 2(2), Monograph 6.

Ricoeur, P. (1980) Narrative Time. In: *On Narrative.* W. J. T. Mitchell (Ed.) Chicago: The University Of Chicago Press. Pp. 165-186.

Saari, C. (1986a), The created relationship: Transference, countertransference and the therapeutic culture. *Clinical Social Work Jour,* 14(1):39-51.

Saari, C. (1986b), The use of metaphor in therapeutic communication with young adolescents. *Child & Adol Social Work Jour,* 3 (1):15-25.

Saari, C. (1988), Interpretation: Event or Process? *Clinical Social Work Jour* 16(4):355-377.

Saari, C. (1991), *The Creation of Meaning in Clinical Social Work.* New York: The Guilford Press.

Saleeby, D. (1994), Culture, theory, and narrative: The intersection of meanings in practice. *Social Work,* 39(4):351-359.

Sarbin, T. R. (1986) The narrative as a root metaphor for psychology. In: Sarbin, T. R. (Ed.) *Narrative Psychology: The storied nature of human conduct.* New York: Praeger. Pp. 3-21.

Schafer, R., (1968), *Aspects of Internalization.* New York: International Universities Press.

Schafer, R. (1980), Narration In The Psychoanalytic Dialogue. In: *On Narrative.* Mitchell, W. J. T. (Ed.) Chicago: The University Of Chicago Press. Pp. 25-50.

Schafer, R. (1981), *Narrative Actions In Psychoanalysis.* Worchester, Mass.: Clark University Press.

Schafer, R. (1983), *The Analytic Attitude.* New York: Basic Books, Inc.

Schafer, R. (1992), *Retelling A Life: Narration And Dialogue In Psychoanalysis.* Basic Books.

Scholes, R. (1980), Language, Narrative And Anti-Narrative. In: *On Narrative.* W. J. T. Mitchell (Ed.) Chicago: The University Of Chicago Press. Pp. 200-208.

Scholes, R., & Kellogg, R. (1966), *The Nature Of Narrative.* London: Oxford University Press.

Sherwood, M. (1969), *The Logic of Explanation in Psychoanalysis.* New York: Academic Press.

Spence, D. P. (1982), *Narrative truth and historical truth.* New York: W.W.Norton.

Spence, D. P. (1987), *The Freudian metaphor: Toward paradigm change in psychoanalysis.* New York: W.W. Norton.

Spence, D. P. (1990), *The Rhetorical Voice Of Psychoanalysis. J. Am Psychoanalytic Assoc* 38(38): 579-605.

Stern, D. N. (1988), The Dialectic Between The "Interpersonal" And The "Intrapsychic": With Particular Emphasis On The Role Of Memory And Representation. *Psychoanalytic Inquiry* 8(4): 505-512.

Stern, D. N. (1989), The representation of relational patterns: developmental considerations. In: *Relationship Disturbances in early Childhood: A Developmental Approach.* Emde, R. N., and Sameroff, A., (Eds.) New York: Basic Books. Pp. 52-69.

Tolpin, M. (1978), Self-objects & oedipal objects: a crucial developmental distinction. *The Psychoanalytic Study of the Child*, 33,167-186.

White, H. (1980), The Value Of Narrativity In The Representation Of Reality. In: *On Narrative.* Mitchell, W. J. T. (Ed.) Chicago: The University Of Chicago Press. pp. 1-24.

Chapter 3

Deconstruction and Reconstruction: A Self-Psychological Perspective on the Construction of Meaning in Psychoanalysis

Maria T. Miliora
Richard B. Ulman

SUMMARY. The authors present and elaborate their thesis that psychoanalysis is a hermeneutic science concerned with the causal nature of meaning. They contend that psychoanalysis is concerned primarily with uncovering the meaning of experience as unconsciously determined, that is, caused, by fantasy and as revealed by symptomatic effects. The cause-and-effect interrelationship that exists among fantasy, meaning, and symptom derives from certain abnormal experiences of self relative to selfobject that occur during early development. The authors draw upon their clinical studies of patients diagnosed with panic disorder, OCD, and OCPD and present two clinical vignettes for illustrative purposes. Using a combined method of "analytic deconstruction" and reconstruction, the authors demon-

---

Maria T. Miliora, PhD, MSW, LCSW, is a psychotherapist and psychoanalyst in private practice and Professor at Suffolk University, Boston, MA. Richard B. Ulman, PhD, is a psychoanalyst in private practice in New York City and Croton-on-Hudson, NY, and a senior faculty member of the Training and Research Institute for Self Psychology.

[Haworth co-indexing entry note]: "Deconstruction and Reconstruction: A Self-Psychological Perspective on the Construction of Meaning in Psychoanalysis." Miliora, Maria T., and Richard B. Ulman. Co-published simultaneously in *Journal of Analytic Social Work* (The Haworth Press, Inc.) Vol. 3, No. 2/3, 1996, pp. 61-81; and: *Narration and Therapeutic Action: The Construction of Meaning in Psychoanalytic Social Work* (ed: Jerrold R. Brandell) The Haworth Press, Inc., 1996, pp. 61-81. Single or multiple copies of this article are available from The Haworth Document Delivery Service [1-800-342-9678, 9:00 a.m. - 5:00 p.m. (EST) E-mail address: get info@haworth.com].

61

strate how various psychopathological states are reflective of failures to transform archaic narcissistic fantasies that unconsciously determine the meaning of the symptoms suffered by those diagnosed with these specific self-disorders. *[Article copies available from The Haworth Document Delivery Service: 1-800-342-9678. E-mail address: getinfo@haworth.com].*

Recently, psychoanalysis, both as a theory and as a practice, has come under critical scrutiny from theoreticians and practitioners alike. Some, like the philosopher of science Grunbaum (1984), challenge its status as a legitimate science (see Wax, 1995, for a critique of Grunbaum's position), while others, like Edelson (1975, 1984, 1988), defend its status as a science. However, both Grunbaum and Edelson have been extremely critical of the theoretical foundations of psychoanalysis.

Others, such as Schafer (1976, 1978, 1992) and Spence (1982, 1994), have called into serious question the actual practice of psychoanalysis as a clinical enterprise. In essence, practitioners like Schafer and Spence question the nature of analytic data and the way in which it is collected and analyzed. They suggest that over the years the methods of data collection and analysis have become the handmaidens of theory, and thus, from a strict methodological point of view, are compromised. The practice of data collection itself is so tied to theory as to be somewhat useless in proving or disproving the theory.

The common denominator behind the critical views of those with such otherwise divergent positions as Grunbaum, Edelson, Schafer, and Spence is a shared belief that psychoanalytic theory has overtaken psychoanalytic practice to the extent that all analytic discourse is becoming circular and tautological. (See also Wolstein, 1985 for a summary of the views of Edelson, Grunbaum, Schafer, and Spence.)

The questioning of these and other critics concerns the basic and fundamental issue of whether psychoanalysis is actually about cause-and-effect or about meaning. There is an assumption on the part of all of these critics that the notions of cause-and-effect versus meaning are, by definition, mutually exclusive. Based on this assumption, it follows that psychoanalysis can be conceived of as either: (1) a science like all other sciences that is concerned with illuminating the nature of cause-and-effect between or among variables, or (2) a hermeneutic discipline concerned with discovering the meaning of experience as revealed through language.

Few of the critics of psychoanalysis have seriously entertained the possibility that the supposed dichotomy between cause-and-effect and meaning is false. If the categories of cause and meaning are actually compatible, then psychoanalysis might be legitimately conceived of as a hermeneutic science concerned with the cause-and-effect of meaning. In positing such a conceptualization, we are building on the unpublished work of Ulman and Zimmermann (1985, 1987) who distinguished psychoanalysis as a social science from the natural sciences. Ulman and Zimmermann view psychoanalysis as concerned primarily with how the unconscious meaning of fantasy serves as a cause with effects in the form of symptoms and psychopathology. Following the philosopher of science von Wright (1971), Ulman and Zimmermann argued in favor of a psychoanalytic view of meaning as causal or causative.

The work of Ulman and Zimmermann serves as a heuristic bridge between those who debate about whether psychoanalysis is best viewed as part of a so-called "narrative tradition" (Spence, 1994) and others who debate about whether psychoanalysis is a science or a hermeneutic. Implicit in the work of Ulman and Zimmermann is the idea that psychoanalysis is part of the narrative tradition while also being a hermeneutic science. It is narrative because it entails the interpretation of the meaning of the story told by symptoms in the language of the unconscious. It is hermeneutic and scientific because it involves the establishment and validation of the causal meaning and effect of fantasy.

Brook (1995), in support of the position of Ulman and Zimmermann, has presented his view that psychoanalysis is "both hermeneutic *and* causal" (p. 523). Illustrating his thesis via clinical material, Brook argued that "reasons can also be causes" (p. 525) and thus meaning and causality are interrelated. (See also Gill, 1991, who maintained that psychoanalysis is a hermeneutic science.)

It is not easy to bridge the discursive chasm separating those who debate about the place of meaning in the conceptualization of psychoanalysis. We attempt to span this gulf by positing that psychoanalysis, as theory and practice, is about the therapeutic dialogue that takes place between patient and analyst regarding the unconscious meaning of the patient's life as revealed by symptom and fantasy. (See Leavy, 1980, for a view of psychoanalysis as an analytic dialogue.) As a therapeutic investigation of the causal meaning of fantasy and its symptomatic effects, psychoanalysis must have a theory of the mind and of human nature that is based on actual clinical practice. If a particular conceptualization of psychoanalysis loses touch with actual clinical practice—as has often been the case in the debates about the best conceptualization of psychoanalysis— then the theoretical discourse becomes too abstract and reified. We believe that practice must determine theory in the case of psychoanalysis. And we maintain that determining how the unconscious meaning of fantasy causes symptoms is an example of the doctrine of the primacy of practice over theory.

In espousing our view, we are returning to Freud's (1908[1907], 1908, 1909[1908]) original thinking about the *meaning* of *symptoms* as revealed by the analysis of *unconscious fantasy*. In so doing, we are following the lead of Ricoeur (1970). Ricoeur was one of the first and is still one of the foremost proponents of a view of Freudian psychoanalysis as a hermeneutic enterprise concerned with the unconscious meaning of symptoms and fantasy.

However, unlike others such as Mackay (1989) and Strenger (1991), both of whom have followed Ricoeur's lead but only implicitly, we explicitly base ourselves on Ricoeur's pioneering re-interpretation of the Freudian corpus. (See Bouchard, 1995, for an appraisal of the value of Ricoeur's work in the context of the current debate about psychoanalysis as a hermeneutic.) In addition, we also proceed from an explicitly self-psychological perspective based on Kohut's (1978[1959],1991[1981]) original contribution to psychoanalytic theory and practice.

Kohut made a number of important clinical discoveries that are especially relevant to our position. In the context of his analytic work with a series of narcissistically disturbed patients, Kohut realized that his unconscious meaning for them was not determined on the basis of his existence as a separate and autonomous person, whom they either loved or hated, but rather was based on his psychological functioning for them as a part of their own psychic structure. Kohut claimed that he served transferentially for these patients as a selfobject, that is, a fantastic part of the self that by magic extends the power and influence of the self in ways otherwise not feasible or possible.

Kohut concluded that on a transference level his patients created an unconscious fantasy (a selfobject fantasy or fantasized selfobject) in which they imagined and experienced him functioning to provide them with desperately needed narcissistic sustenance. Such vital nurturance was possible in one of two forms: (1) the reflection back or *mirroring* on the part of the analyst of patients' highly inflated sense of their own grandiosity; or, (2) the extension by the analyst of patients' exalted or *idealized* sense of their omnipotence. Kohut referred respectively to these two transference paradigms as mirroring of the archaic grandiose self and idealization of the omnipotent parent imago. These two unconscious fantasy constellations were the main forms of what Kohut viewed as archaic narcissism, which under adverse and unempathic conditions remains in a developmentally arrested state.

In elaborating his psychoanalytic theory of the self or self psychology,

Kohut argued originally that a specific set of unconscious fantasies, which were typical expressions of archaic narcissism, organize the subjective experience of persons suffering from a narcissistic personality disorder or self disorder. (See Ulman & Brothers, 1988 for a discussion of fantasy in the early work of Kohut.) According to Kohut, such individuals organize experience and imbue it with its personal meaning on the basis of the operation of a narcissistic prism that skews both cognition and affect in a particular symptomatic direction. These individuals were so archaically organized, Kohut contended, that they were especially prone to serious disturbances in self-esteem regulation. He characterized these narcissistic disturbances in terms of a cluster of symptoms including empty and depleted depression, disintegration anxiety, loneliness, and narcissistic rage. More specifically, he claimed that these types of narcissistic pathology gave expression symptomatically to serious disturbances in unconscious fantasies of the self in relation to the selfobject. The meaning of experience, in these instances, could be understood empathically, therefore, on the basis of analyzing the impact of these "central organizing fantasies" (Nurnberg & Shapiro, 1983, p. 493) on the person.

We also have incorporated Beres and Arlow's (1974) work on the fantasy-based nature of empathy as well as Margulies' (1989) idea of "empathic imagination." We adopt an analytic stance based on the technique of analyzing the unconscious meaning of fantasy as revealed by symptom. We contend that such an analytic posture is reflective of Kohut's understanding of the empathic-introspective mode of observation. According to Kohut (1971), this analytic mode of listening involves the analyst occupying an "imaginary point inside the psychic organization of the individual with whose introspection he empathically identifies" (p. 219, footnote 8). Ultimately, it is the patient who fantasizes unconsciously and thereby creates the meaning of symptoms. In the context of the analytic setting, it is then possible for the patient to introspect about such meaning and for the analyst to employ "empathic imagination" to understand this meaning.

We rely on introspection and empathy as the two primary and interrelated modes of observation by which to make sense, that is, arrive at meaning, in the context of the "psychoanalytic dialogue"(Leavy,1980). Utilizing Kohut's notion of introspection and empathy, we follow the work of Ulman and Brothers (1988) who developed what they called the "applied psychoanalytic research technique of empathic or vicarious introspection" (p. 28). We are also pursuing the work of Ulman and Brothers as well as Ulman and Paul (1989, 1990, 1992) in exploring the cause-and-effect interrelationship that we posit as existing among fantasy, meaning, and symptom.

Ulman and his coworkers built on the previous work of Ulman and Stolorow (1985) in examining this interrelationship in the clinical context of post traumatic stress disorder (PTSD) and addiction. Ulman and Stolorow developed the intersubjective concept of the "transference-countertransference neurosis" as an analytic means of illuminating the inevitable, clinical intermingling of the subjectivities of both patient and analyst. According to Ulman and Stolorow, patient and analyst are to varying degrees organized subjectively by "archaic structures" that codetermine for both participants the unconscious meaning of the analytic experience.

Ulman and Brothers (1988) advanced the idea of the transference-countertransference neurosis by placing what they termed "archaic narcissistic fantasy" (p. 9) at the center of this intersubjective configuration. Following the early work of Kohut, they defined these fantasies as involving magical illusions of mirrored grandiosity (that is, an imaginary scenario in which the person envisions an exhibitionistic display before an admiring audience) or idealized merger with the omnipotent (that is, an imaginary scenario in which the person pictures being joined to or with an all-powerful or all-knowing presence).

Within the intersubjective context of the transference-countertransference neurosis, Ulman and Brothers (1988) reconstructed analytically the unconscious meaning of traumatic experiences of rape, incest, and combat. These authors argued that such traumatic meaning is determined unconsciously or caused by the shattering and faulty restoration of these archaic narcissistic fantasies. Moreover, they contended that the traumatic meaning of such shattering and faulty restoration is expressed symptomatically in the re-experiencing and numbing symptoms of PTSD. It is implicit in their work that the deconstruction of the meaning of the PTSD symptoms leads to the reconstruction of the significance of the traumatic experience.

Ulman and Paul (1989, 1990, 1992) furthered the work of Ulman and Brothers as well as Ulman and Stolorow. Ulman and Paul utilized the intersubjective field as a clinical means of understanding empathically the unconscious, phantasmagorical meaning of the addictive experience. In treating the symptoms of addiction—including alcoholism, drug abuse, eating disorders, and compulsive gambling—Ulman and Paul developed the therapeutic process of intersubjective absorption. They discovered that the addicted patient relied on various things and activities (termed "addictive trigger mechanisms" or "ATMs") as a means of activating otherwise latent archaic narcissistic fantasies. When manifest in consciousness and subjective awareness, these fantasies usher in a blissful state of dissociation and anesthetization that counteracts temporarily and partially the psychic pain associated with dysphoric affects. The unconscious meaning of the addictive experience can be understood empathically, according to Ulman and Paul, by analyzing the significance of the symptomatic action of "dissociative anesthetization."

In working with the addicted patient, Ulman and Paul took advantage of the selfobject transference as a means of therapeutically absorbing the (faulty) psychological functioning of the symptoms of addiction. In other words, these authors postulate that the analyst is fantasized transferentially by the patient as the clinical equivalent to an ATM. By facilitating such a therapeutic transference fantasy, the analyst helps addicted patients to wean themselves gradually off ATMs and onto the selfobject functioning of the analyst. And, unlike the faulty functioning of ATMs, the selfobject functioning of the analyst can be internalized and transmuted in the form of building psychic structure.

We (Miliora & Ulman 1994, 1995) have taken the idea of Ulman and Paul of intersubjective absorption and applied it to the diagnostic entities of panic disorder and obsessive-compulsive disorder (OCD). We employed the intersubjective field, as co-determined by the respective subjectivities of patient and analyst, as an analytic medium in which to reconstruct the personal meaning of certain abnormal experiences from the past. These experiences were expressed symptomatically in the form of panic disorder and OCD, and were determined unconsciously or caused by particular archaic narcissistic fantasies. More specifically, we found that a fantasy of imperviousness and containment determined the symptoms of panic disorder, whereas a fantasy of omniscience and infallibility caused the symptoms of OCD.

In the case of panic disorder, we refined the therapeutic process of intersubjective absorption as a means of containing clinically the dysphoric affect (which we term "diffusion" anxiety) associated with panic. Gradually, the panic-disordered patient becomes more self-contained as a result of intersubjective absorption, and hence is less prone to panicking.

In the case of OCD, we modified intersubjective absorption and devised a related therapeutic process of intersubjective osmosis. Clinically, the OCD patient embraces the analyst transferentially as an imaginary mediator who is capable of magically deciphering the meaning of experience. On the basis of this selfobject transference fantasy, the OCD patient develops slowly a more accurate and reliable capacity for processing information from within and without and hence creating order out of chaos.

We believe that our analytic discoveries constitute a significant self-psychological contribution to the idea that psychoanalysis is a hermeneutic science. As such, it is concerned primarily with the unconscious meaning of experience as determined by fantasy and as revealed by symptom. Our work represents, therefore, a self-psychological return to Freud's early fantasy-based model of psychopathology. And, like Freud's original model, our fantasy-based model of psychopathology rests on diagnostic and symptom specificity. In other words, it relies on particular diagnostic entities with distinctive symptoms.

However, there is a major difference between the classical view of Freud and our self-psychological perspective. Freud viewed fantasy primarily in terms of psychosexual and aggressive drives in conflict with other psychic forces. Essentially, we conceive of fantasy in terms of archaic narcissistic illusions. In psychopathological disorders like panic and OCD, these magical illusions either have failed to undergo sufficient developmental transformation or have remained in various states of developmental arrest.

Finally, our work constitutes an advance in psychoanalytic hermeneutics. It utilizes a technique of *analytic deconstruction* of the psychic significance of symptoms as a way of *reconstructing* the phantasmagorical meaning of abnormal and often traumatic experiences of the past.

PANIC DISORDER

We used the fourth edition of the *Diagnostic and Statistical Manual* (DSM-IV, 1994) as the clinical basis for our self-psychological study of a series of ten (10) panic-disordered patients who were treated over the course of a number of years. We employed the approach of Ulman et al., whereby we sought to establish the unconscious meaning of the symptoms of panic by way of the analysis of various selfobject transference fantasies.

There are many current studies in the field of biological psychiatry (see, for example, Klein, 1964, 1981; Klein et al., 1985; Quitkin et al., 1972; Shear, 1988; Telch, 1988; Swinson & Kuch, 1990; and Klerman et al., 1993) that point to a significant and particular biochemical abnormality in the brain functioning of those patients suffering from panic disorder. Based on this finding, a number of specific psychopharmacological drug therapies have been developed for the treatment of panic disorder. As a result, many in the mental health field now believe (incorrectly, we contend) that psychopharmacology is the therapy of choice in the treatment of panic disorder.

However, there is a rich analytic literature dating back to Deutsch (1929), continuing with Frances and Dunn (1975), and culminating most recently with Silber (1989) indicating that the analysis and working through of various unconscious fantasies is crucial to the effective treatment of panic disorder. Based on our analytic experience, we believe that although medication is often necessary in treating panic disorder, it is not sufficient. The psychopharmacological reduction of the florid symptoms of panic disorder should only pave the way for an analytic exploration of the nature of the unconscious fantasy (of imperviousness and containment) which, we maintain, determines the symptomatic meaning of the experience of panicking. Without appropriate analytic work, the panic-disordered patient remains organized unconsciously in accordance with archaic narcissistic fantasies, and hence is still vulnerable psychologically to future episodes of panic.

We discovered that the disorienting and dissociative symptoms of panic disorder, many of which are physiological in nature, were actually a psychological expression of the pathological disturbance of a blissful fantasy of psychic imperviousness. Unconsciously, the panic disordered person imagines and fantasizes being immune or impenetrable to all forms of emotional distress, painful sensations, and noxious environmental stimuli in general. It is *as if* such persons believed unconsciously that they existed in a boundless container or super-fortified receptacle that protected them psychologically from all forms of painful emotions and discomforting sensations. One of our panic patients described himself as a "wall that nothing could penetrate." Another patient (see the case of Ellie, below) reported needing to be "strong" and always "happy" even as a young child so as not to appear to her parents to be a "whiner." Still another of our panic-disordered patients liked to imagine herself as having been "impervious" to the highly charged emotional distress that occurred between her parents during her childhood. Finally, one of our panic-disordered patients imagined herself as being like a duck in that she could let any and all disturbing experiences magically roll off her back like water off a duck.

The fantasy of imperviousness expresses archaic narcissism. In this sense, panic-disordered persons fantasize themselves as impervious to emotional onslaughts even when situations occur that appropriately *should* distress them. Archaic narcissistic fantasies originate in early childhood experiences with caretakers functioning as selfobjects. Sometimes, these archaic fantasies have failed to undergo sufficient developmental transformation. As a result, they have not been tempered and modulated by experience. Consequently, they retain a primitive, highly unrealistic, phantasmagorical meaning. In addition, these fantasies are fragile and therefore are easily disturbed. In other words, the unconscious meaning of these fantasies can change dramatically from narcissistic bliss to narcissistic mortification.

Being organized unconsciously in accordance with such a powerful yet volatile fantasy leaves the panic-prone individual vulnerable to the loss of a magical illusion of imperviousness and a resulting state of panic. Specifically, if the fantasy of imperviousness is disturbed, such an individual experiences a painful sense of diffusion and loss of personal boundedness. In addition, there is a flood of overwhelming emotions and breakdown of normal forms of self-control. In the context of this kind of abnormal experience, the panic-ridden individual no longer has a sense of self as organized unconsciously around a fantasy of imperviousness. Instead, the panic-ridden person fantasizes the self as diffuse, unbounded, and like a sieve or colander. In a state of panic, the meaning of experience is now organized unconsciously by a mortifying fantasy of being sieve-like.

On the basis of such a dreadful fantasy, the panicky person's sense of self undergoes a dramatic, often unexpected, and sudden change in relation to the selfobject milieu. A pathological alteration occurs which is accompanied by a loss of control over many normal physiologic functions including perspiration, as well as evacuation and elimination. In addition to heart palpitations, sweaty palms, and loss of control over bladder and sphincter, there are dissociative symptoms including depersonalization, derealization, and disembodiment.

We used an analytic method whereby we deconstructed the psychic significance of these physiologic and psychogenic symptoms as a means of reconstructing the unconscious meaning of early childhood fantasies. We realized that, in the case of the panic-disordered patient, a derailment had occurred in the normal unfolding and developmental transformation of selfobject fantasies of parents as boundless containers, and corresponding fantasies of the self as impervious.

This fantasy matrix of self and selfobject can be viewed developmentally as the precursor to the mature functional capacity for self-containment. In effect, the functional capacity for self-containment is faulty or lacking in the psychic repertoire of panic-disordered patients. Archaic fantasies or illusions of cohesiveness enable panic-disordered patients to maintain a semblance of organization in their subjective worlds. As a substitute for missing or faulty self-structure, these fantasies constitute defensive illusions serving to prop up and brace otherwise fragile, psychic boundaries.

The failure on the part of the panic-prone child to adequately transform these self-state and selfobject fantasies results in a pathological tendency to organize the unconscious meaning of personal experience in accordance with fragile and precarious illusions of imperviousness and boundlessness. These illusions are easily disturbed as evidenced, later in life, by the emergence of a full-blown panic disorder.

Clinical Vignette

Ellie, a thirty-six-year-old single woman, entered treatment because she had suffered from spontaneous and unexpected panic attacks for the previous three months. The attacks included heart palpitations, sweating, sinking feelings in her abdomen, derealization, and a fear that she was dying.

Ellie formed a spontaneous selfobject transference that included both mirroring and idealizing dimensions. Her dream material included images of structures such as houses and apartments. In the dream-fantasy, she felt safe and contained. Other dream images included her being chosen as special by the analyst whom she pictured as a wise woman.

On a more conscious level, Ellie described her relationship with the analyst as helping her to feel secure. During those periods when Ellie was in the throes of panic attacks, she telephoned the analyst and left messages describing her experience of panic. Ellie explained that contacting the analyst by phone provided her with relief from the experience of panic. It became clear that Ellie had a transference fantasy of the analyst-as-selfobject that served as a boundless container. This transference fantasy helped her avoid panicking.

Ellie described her childhood as one in which she never felt safe in her home with her parents and siblings. Ellie's mother was described as very anxious. At a young age, Ellie learned that her normal feelings of anxiousness and fear were neither acknowledged nor relieved by her parents. In other words, her parents, in their role as idealized selfobjects, did not contain these unpleasant feelings, and, consequently, did not help Ellie achieve a capacity for self-containment. As a matter of fact, unpleasant emotions made her parents anxious, and, if Ellie shared such feelings with them, they immediately sought to change the emotional meaning of her experience.

In order to please her parents, Ellie learned to adopt a facade of happiness and of being without unpleasant feelings. This happy facade was an expression of a fantasy of being impervious to emotional distress. Concurrently, Ellie became over-involved in the emotional lives of other family members and friends. Later, and as an adult, Ellie manifested signs of being a workaholic in a demanding professional job. When she felt overwhelmed, she experienced herself as diffuse and boundary-less. Ellie abused marijuana on a daily basis during her adolescence and through her twenties and early thirties. Soon after she stopped using pot on a regular basis, the panic attacks began.

During four years of twice weekly analytic therapy, Ellie and the analyst came to understand that Ellie had defined herself unconsciously in terms of a fantasy of being "strong" and thereby impervious to disturbing emotions and bodily sensations. Using pot had enabled her to defend against feeling overwhelmed, diffuse, and boundary-less. When she stopped using pot, the panic attacks began as a direct response to her limited capacity for self-containment.

The psychic significance of the symptoms of panic was deconstructed as indicative of a fantasy of imperviousness. The symptoms arose in the context of Ellie's limited capacity for self-containment. The fantasy was a rudimentary precursor for this capacity, a way for her to contend with a feeling of being overwhelmed. When she was overwhelmed by emotional distress in her surroundings, Ellie experienced herself as diffuse and boundary-less. In other words, based on this fantasy of narcissistic mortification, Ellie imagined herself as being sieve-like. This fantasy was the opposite, or flipside, of the blissful fantasy of imperviousness.

The selfobject fantasy of the analyst as a limitless receptacle or boundless container enabled Ellie to use the analyst as a depository for her panicky feelings. Her transference fantasy also served as a crude precursor for her still limited capacity for self-containment. The containing selfobject function of the analyst operated in sessions as Ellie related experiences that left her feeling "edgy" and "drained." Ellie spoke of her dread that these feelings signaled an impending panic attack. The analyst remained calm in the face of Ellie's agitation (that is, "diffusion" anxiety) and absorbed these feelings. The analyst thus contained the agitation and she gave Ellie the message that the anxiousness was not to be feared as an indicator of impending catastrophe and a panic attack.

When the analyst responded back to Ellie, she, in effect, enabled Ellie to reabsorb the now detoxified dysphoric affect in a more tolerable form. This process of intersubjective absorption, repeated many times even during a session, helped Ellie to internalize and transmute the analyst's containing function. As a consequence, Ellie became progressively less afraid of her feelings. This enabled Ellie to expand her capacity and tolerance for feelings, and thereby she expanded her capacity for self-containment.

The process of intersubjective absorption occurred in the context of Ellie's transference fantasy and its meaning to Ellie that she was impervious, as the analyst was a boundless container. While this process of intersubjective absorption was active and on-going, the symptoms of panic diminished. This selfobject fantasy underwent therapeutic transformation during the period of analytic treatment. Ultimately, it was transmutingly internalized in the form of Ellie's increased capacity for self-containment. With the selfobject transference in effect, it was possible to reconstruct the unconscious meaning of the fantasy of imperviousness and to place it in its original genetic context.

After five years of self-psychological analysis, Ellie had not had a panic attack in more than a year. She evolved into a woman capable of emotional expression, a greatly improved sense of her personal boundaries, and an expanded capacity for self-containment.

In summary, we took Ellie's panic symptoms very seriously. We did not reduce them to mere epiphenomena with little clinical significance. Analytically, we deconstructed the meaning of these symptoms in this and other cases. In so doing, we discovered a Janus-faced fantasy system that determined, that is, caused the unconscious meaning of a significant domain of self-experience for the panic-ridden person.

OCD

Again relying on the analytic technique introduced originally by Ulman et al., we have explored the fantasy-based meaning of the symptoms of OCD. As was the case in our self-psychological study of panic disorder, this investigation studied 10 OCD patients who were treated over the course of a number of years of analytic therapy. These patients were chosen for inclusion in the study on the basis of meeting the DSM-IV (1994) diagnostic criteria for either OCD or the related clinical entity of obsessive-compulsive personality disorder (OCPD). In a fashion similar to our study of panic disorder, we conducted our investigation without any initial or preconceived notion of the exact nature of the fantasy system that we suspected determined the unconscious meaning of the OCD symptoms. However, we had some basis for our suspicions from the long line of analytic work dating back to Freud (1895[1894], 1909, 1913) and Ferenczi (1956[1913]), continuing with Lewin (1939) and Mahler-Schoenberger (1942), and culminating most recently with Eigen (1989), indicating that omniscience (and infallibility) as well as its opposite, "pseudostupidity," are crucial to understanding and treating obsessive-compulsivity.

In the analytic context of transference fantasies of mirroring and idealization, we realized that our OCD and OCPD patients experienced or imagined us as selfobjects that served a mediating function. In other words, these patients looked to us to ascertain and discern the meaning of experience, both as it originated internally from within the mind and body and as it sprang externally from outside in the environment. Such experiences are based on actual events as well as on the reactions of other people. More specifically, the deconstruction of the psychic significance of the OCD symptoms revealed that these OCD patients had fantasized us as endowed with a magical power of omniscience. In other words, they imagined us as infallible. (We distinguish omniscience from omnipotence which involves a fantasy of the other as all-powerful. Omniscience or infallibility is about supernatural mental or psychic power, whereas omnipotence is about superhuman physical strength and powers.)

Over the course of long-term analytic treatment, we found that the OCD and OCPD symptoms decreased as these unconscious fantasies of omniscience and infallibility increasingly organized our patients' transference experience. We realized that these symptoms–including obsessive ruminations, cogitations, doubt, ambivalence, and worrying as well as compulsive doing and undoing, cleanliness, and perfectionistic ordering–were the expressions of pathological disturbance in patients' fantasies of their own omniscience and infallibility.

We came to understand that as children these patients had failed to sufficiently endow parents as selfobjects, with the power of omniscience and the capacity to mediate the meaning of experience. Usually, these failures took place in the developmental context of parents who were unable to appreciate empathically a child's normal need for an omniscient and infallible presence. Thus, these patients had been forced as children to retain the illusion of their own omniscience. As a result, they imagined and fantasized that they were all-knowing, and hence knew the right and perfect order of everything in their immediate surroundings. Lacking in early life the presence of an infallible other to mediate the meaning of experience these individuals were required to assume for themselves such an ability.

The archaic fantasies of omniscience and infallibility can be viewed developmentally as untransformed versions of the psychic capacity for reliably knowing the meaning of one's own experience. We refer to this as the development of a "noetic self." The noetic self consists of a mature capacity to process information in such a way as to ascertain and discern the meaning of experience. It is this cognitive capacity that is missing or faulty in the psychic repertoire of OCD and OCPD patients.

These patients base their sense of self on a fragile and precarious fantasy of personal omniscience. As a result, they leave themselves vulnerable to constantly feeling just the opposite, namely, they imagine themselves as imbeciles or morons who know nothing and lack any sense of the right order of things. The desperate yet ultimately futile attempt to restore a sense of infallibility was reflected symptomatically in obsessive thought patterns and compulsive behaviors. The meaning of experience was organized unconsciously for the OCD-person by the dialectical action of a Janus-faced fantasy system. It vacillated wildly between a blissful sense of knowing all and ordering everything and a dreadful sense of knowing nothing and of being unable to order anything.

In summary, the fantasy system of the OCD patient vacillates between blissful versions of omniscience and perfect order and mortifying visions of imbecility and chaos. It is the equivalent of the fantasy system of the panic-disordered patient which vacillates between blissful visions of imperviousness and containment and mortifying visions of diffusion and boundlessness.

Clinical Vignette

Eli, a thirty-eight-year-old twice divorced man entered analytic therapy because of severe and debilitating obsessive-compulsive symptoms. He was virtually housebound as a result of obsessive worrying and compulsive checking. He met all of the DSM-IV diagnostic criteria for obsessive-compulsive disorder.

During the early phase of treatment, Eli resisted forming a selfobject transference to the analyst. This resistance derived from a specific dread. Eli's father had been seriously ill during most of Eli's childhood and had died when Eli was a teenager. As a result, Eli lacked an effective paternal presence to help him mediate the meaning of experience during his childhood and adolescence. Consequently, he had been unable to transpose onto his father an archaic fantasy of his own omniscience. As a result, Eli remained arrested developmentally in the process of transforming such a magical illusion into a mature sense of the range and limits of his own knowledge. In other words, he did not have a mature sense of himself as knowledgeable, that is, as a noetic self. For Eli there were only two polar opposite possibilities: either he knew all and could put everything in its proper place, or he knew nothing and was forced to leave everything in chaos. In other words, Eli imagined either that he was omniscient and had his personal world in perfect order or that he was an imbecile whose personal world was in total disarray.

It was possible, based on Eli's fantasy of omniscience, to deconstruct the meaning of his obsessive-compulsive symptoms. Because of the fragile nature of this archaic fantasy, Eli was vulnerable constantly to feeling that he was totally ignorant of the right and wrong order. His symptoms were manifestations of his desperate yet futile attempts to maintain or restore the fantasies of infallibility and the perfect order whenever these fantasies were seriously disturbed.

Eli resisted forming a selfobject transference to the analyst because he dreaded allowing the analyst to become the long sought after and desired father who could serve as an omniscient mediator of the meaning of experience. He neither trusted nor believed in the real possibility of an infallible presence other than himself. He dreaded giving up reliance on his own fantastic ability to know and order everything perfectly for fear of being once again disappointed as he had in the past.

In order to reduce the resistance, the analyst had to reconstruct the unconscious meaning of the fantasy of Eli's dread to repeat the traumatic past. (See A. Ornstein, 1974, 1991 on the self-psychological understanding of the dread to repeat.) Over time, the analyst helped Eli understand his dread and Eli lessened his resistance to forming a selfobject transference based on a fantasy of omniscience. Gradually, Eli began to experience the analyst transferentially as a fantasied, infallible figure. Eli asked questions incessantly of the analyst; the analyst attempted to answer them as best as possible. In utilizing the analyst's answers on a tentative and provisional basis, however, Eli was learning through (intersubjective) osmosis, as it were, how to arrive at his own answers. He held onto the answers provided him by the analyst only as long as was needed to decipher his own right from wrong, good from bad, correct from incorrect.

In allowing the analyst to mediate the meaning of experience in the form of accepting the analyst's answers to his questions, Eli had created a transference fantasy of the analyst as an idealized selfobject that functioned as an auxiliary information processing center. As such, the analyst replaced and took over for Eli's faulty and limited ability to process information accurately and reliably.

In the early stages of the analysis, Eli depended almost totally on the analyst as an auxiliary center for processing information. His use of the analyst in this noetic capacity enabled him to develop his own ability to decipher the meaning of experience. He freed himself gradually from his previous pathological entanglement in obsessive thinking and compulsive behavior, both of which were the symptomatic expression of the meaning of experience as organized unconsciously by archaic narcissistic fantasies.

Over the years, however, Eli has been able to borrow at first the analyst's mediating function, and subsequently to make it his own. Thus, in the language of self psychology, Eli has internalized and transmuted the analyst as an omniscient selfobject. In the process of building his own psychic structure in the form of an enhanced information processing capacity, Eli has learned through intersubjective osmosis to better trust his own assessments, perceptions, judgements, and intuitions. In so doing, he has alleviated significantly his tendency toward obsessive-compulsivity, made necessary in the past because of his pathological doubt, uncertainty, and ambivalence.

CONCLUSION

In summary, our recent work on panic disorder as well as OCD and OCPD marks a significant self-psychological contribution to the contention that psychoanalysis is a hermeneutic science concerned with the interpretation and analysis of the unconscious meaning of experience. Our findings demonstrate that the meaning of certain abnormal experiences from the past has significance in the present, especially when viewed in terms of specific diagnostic entities with particular symptomatology.

Moreover, we presented clinical data in support of our view that fantasies have an unconscious meaning as derived from early experiences of self and selfobject that consequently have a cause-and-effect relationship to symptoms. By incorporating both the categories of meaning and causality, we believe that our work demonstrates that psychoanalysis can be conceived of legitimately as a hermeneutic *science.*

Linking our self-psychological thinking with the classical thought of Freud, we sought to correct a tendency among many current defenders of the concept of meaning. We assert that they tend to miss the importance of diagnosis and symptom-formation to understanding personal meaning. Like Freud, we contend that diagnosis and symptomatology are essential to analyzing the unconscious fantasies that determine psychopathology. However, unlike Freud, we do not believe that fantasy need be limited theoretically or practically to the sexual and aggressive drives; rather it may include significant narcissistic sectors of self-experience in relation to selfobject. We described these respectively as self-state and selfobject fantasies that together make up a Janus-faced fantasy system or matrix. We have used a combined method of analytic *deconstruction* and *reconstruction* to understand various psychopathological states such as panic disorder and OCD. Such disorders are reflective of deficits in psychic structure and functioning that determine the unconscious meaning of the symptoms of those suffering from specific self-disorders.

BIBLIOGRAPHY

American Psychiatric Association. (1994). *Diagnostic and Statistical Manual of Mental Disorders*, (DSM-IV). Washington, D.C.: Author.

Beres, D. & Arlow, J. A. (1974). Fantasy and identification in empathy. *Psychoanalytic Quarterly, 43*, 26-50.

Bouchard, M-A. (1995). The specificity of hermeneutics in psychoanalysis: Leaps on the path from construction to recollection. *International Journal of Psychoanalysis, 76*, 533-546.

Brook, A. (1995). Explanation in the hermeneutic science. *International Journal of Psychoanalysis, 76*, 519-532.

Deutsch, H. (1929). The genesis of agoraphobia. *International Journal of Psychoanalysis, X*, 51-69.

Edelson, M. (1975). *Language and Interpretation in Psychoanalysis*. Chicago: The University of Chicago Press.

Edelson, M. (1984). *Hypothesis and Evidence in Psychoanalysis*. Chicago: The University of Chicago Press.

Edelson, M. (1988). *Psychoanalysis: A Theory in Crisis*. Chicago: The University of Chicago Press.

Eigen, M. (1989). Aspects of omniscience. In M. G. Fromm & B. L. Smith (Eds.), *The Facilitating Environment: Clinical Applications of Winnicott's Theory*, pp. 604-628. Madison, CT: International Universities Press.

Ferenczi, S. (1956[1913]). *Sex in Psycho-Analysis* (Contributions to Psycho-Analysis). New York: Dover Publications.

Frances, A. & Dunn, P. (1975). The attachment-autonomy conflict in agoraphobia. *International Journal of Psychoanalysis, 56*, 435-439.

Freud, S. (1895 [1894]). Obsessions and phobias. *Standard Edition, 3*: 74-84. London: Hogarth Press, 1955.

Freud, S. (1908[1907]). Creative writers and day-dreaming. *Standard Edition*, tr. J. Strachey, pp. 143-153. London: Hogarth Press, 1959.

Freud, S. (1908). Hysterical phantasies and their relation to bisexuality. *Standard Edition*, tr. J. Strachey, pp. 159-166. London: Hogarth Press, 1959.

Freud, S. (1909[1908]). Some general remarks on hysterical attacks. *Standard Edition*, tr. J. Strachey, pp. 229-234. London: Hogarth Press, 1959.

Freud, S. (1909). Notes upon a case of obsessional neurosis. *Standard Edition, 10*:153-320. London: Hogarth Press, 1955.

Freud, S. (1913). Totem and taboo. *Standard Edition, 13*: 1-162. London: Hogarth Press, 1955.

Gill, M. (1991). Merton Gill speaks his mind. *The American Psychoanalyst, 25*(1), 17-21.

Grunbaum, A. (1984). *The Foundations of Psychoanalysis*. Berkeley, CA: University of California Press.

Klein, D. F. (1964). Delineation of two drug responsive anxiety syndromes, *Psychopharmacologia, 5*, 397-408.

Klein, D. F. (1981). Anxiety reconceptualized. In D.F. Klein & J. Rabkin (Eds.), *Anxiety: New Research and Changing Concepts*, pp. 235-265. New York: Raven Press.

Klein, D. F., Rabkin, J. G., & Gorman, J. M. (1985). Etiological and pathophysiological inferences from the pharmacological treatment of anxiety. In A. H. Tuma & J. D. Maser (Eds.), *Anxiety and the Anxiety Disorders*, pp. 501-532. Hillsdale, NJ: Lawrence Erlbaum.

Klerman, G. L., Hirschfeld, R. M. A., Weissman, M. M., Pelicier, Y., Ballenger, J. C., Costa E Silva, J. A., Judd, L. L., & Keller, M. B.(Eds.), (1993). *Panic*

Anxiety and Its Treatments, A Task Force Report of the World Psychiatric Association. Washington, DC: American Psychiatric Press.

Kohut, H. (1971). *The Analysis of the Self*. Madison, CT: International Universities Press.

Kohut, H. (1978[1959]). Introspection, empathy, and psychoanalysis. In P. H. Ornstein (Ed.), *The Search for the Self, I*, pp. 205-232. New York: International Universities Press.

Kohut, H. (1991[1981]). Introspection, empathy, and the semicircle of mental health. In P. H. Ornstein (Ed.), *The Search for the Self, 4*, pp. 537-567. Madison, CT: International Universities Press.

Leavy, S. (1980). *The Psychoanalytic Dialogue*. New Haven, CT: Yale University Press.

Lewin, B. D. (1939). Some observations on knowledge, belief and the impulse to know. *The International Journal of Psychoanalysis, 20*, 426-431.

Mackay, N. (1989). *Motivation and Explanation: An Essay on Freud's Philosophy of Science*. Madison, CT: International Universities Press.

Mahler-Schoenberger, M. (1942). Pseudoimbecility: A magic cap of invisibility. *The Psychoanalytic Quarterly, 11*, 149-164.

Margulies, A. (1989). *The Empathic Imagination*. New York: W.W. Norton.

Miliora, M. T. & Ulman, R. B. (1994). Panic disorder: A bioself-psychological perspective. Paper presented at the Second National Clinical Social Work Conference, Washington, D.C., May, 1994. Submitted for publication.

Miliora, M. T. & Ulman, R. B. (1995). Obsessive-compulsive disorder and obsessive-compulsive personality disorder: A bioself-psychological perspective. Paper presented at the Fifth National Clinical Conference, National Membership Committee on Psychoanalysis in Clinical Social Work, New York City, October, 1995.

Nurnberg, H. G. & Shapiro, L. M. (1983). The central organizing fantasy. *Psychoanalytic Review, 70* (4), 493-503.

Ornstein, A. (1974). The dread to repeat and the new beginning: A contribution to the psychoanalytic treatment of narcissistic personality disorders. *The Annual of Psychoanalysis, 2*, 231-248.

Ornstein, A. (1991). The dread to repeat: Comments on the working-through process in psychoanalysis. *Journal of the American Psychoanalytic Association, 39*(2), 377-398.

Quitkin, F. M., Rifkin, A., Kaplan, J. & Klein, D. F. (1972). Phobic anxiety syndrome complicated by drug dependence and addiction. *Archives of General Psychiatry, 27*, 159-162.

Ricoeur, P. (1970). *Freud and Philosophy*. New Haven, CT: Yale University Press.

Schafer, R. (1976). *A New Language for Psychoanalysis*. New Haven, CT: Yale University Press.

Schafer, R. (1978). *Language and Insight*. New Haven, CT: Yale University Press.

Schafer, R. (1992). *Retelling a Life: Narration and Dialogue in Psychoanalysis*. New York: Basic Books.

Shear, K. M. (1988). Cognitive and biological models of panic: Toward an integration. In S. Rachman & J. D. Maser (Eds.), *Panic: Psychological Perspectives*, pp. 51-70. Hillsdale, NJ: Lawrence Erlbaum.

Silber, A. (1989). Panic attacks facilitating recall and mastery: Implications for psychoanalytic technique. *Journal of the American Psychoanalytic Association, 37*, 337-364.

Spence, D. P. (1982). *Narrative Truth and Historical Truth*. New York: W. W. Norton.

Spence, D. P. (1994). *The Rhetorical Voice of Psychoanalysis: Displacement of Evidence by Theory*. Cambridge, MA: Harvard University Press.

Strenger, C. (1991). *Between Hermeneutics and Science: An Essay on the Epistemology of Psychoanalysis*. Monograph 59, *Psychological Issues*. Madison, CT: International Universities Press.

Swinson, R. P. & Kuch, K. (1990). Clinical features of panic and related disorders. In James C. Ballenger (Ed.), *Clinical Aspects of Panic Disorder*, pp. 13-30. New York: Wiley-Liss.

Telch, M. J. (1988). Combined pharmacological and psychological treatments for panic sufferers. In S. Rachman & J. D. Maser (Eds.), *Panic: Psychological Perspectives*, pp. 167-187. Hillsdale, NJ: Lawrence Erlbaum.

Ulman, R. B. & Brothers, D. (1988). *The Shattered Self*. Hillsdale, New Jersey: The Analytic Press.

Ulman, R. B. & Paul, H. (1989). A self-psychological theory and approach to treating substance abuse disorders: The "intersubjective absorption" hypothesis. In A. Goldberg, (Ed.), *Progress in Self Psychology, 5*, pp. 121-141. Hillsdale, New Jersey: The Analytic Press.

Ulman, R. B. & Paul, H.(1990), The addictive personality and "addictive trigger mechanisms"(ATMs): The self psychology of addiction and its treatment. In A. Goldberg (Ed.), *Progress in Self Psychology, 6*, pp.129-156. Hillsdale, New Jersey: The Analytic Press.

Ulman, R. B. & Paul, H. (1992). Dissociative anesthesia and the transitional selfobject transference in the intersubjective treatment of the addictive personality. In A. Goldberg (Ed.), *Progress in Self Psychology, 8*, pp. 109-139. Hillsdale, New Jersey: The Analytic Press.

Ulman, R. B. & Stolorow, R. D. (1985). The "transference-countertransference neurosis in psychoanalysis: An intersubjective viewpoint. *Bulletin of the Menninger Clinic, 49*(1), 37-51.

Ulman, R. B. & Zimmermann, P. B. (1985). Psychoanalysis as a hermeneutic science and the paradigm of subjectivity: A prolegomenon. Paper delivered at the Eighth Annual Meeting of the International Society for Political Psychology, Washington, D.C., June.

Ulman, R. B. & Zimmermann, P. B. (1987). Psychoanalysis as a hermeneutic science and the new paradigm of subjectivity: Evolution of a research tradition. Manuscript presented at the Tenth Annual Scientific Meeting of the International Society of Political Psychology, San Francisco, July.

von Wright, G. H. (1971). *Explanation and Understanding*. Ithaca, NY: Cornell University Press.

Wax, M. L. (1995). How secure are Grunbaum's foundations? *International Journal of Psychoanalysis*, *76*, 547-556.

Wolstein, B. (1985). Restructuring psychoanalysis: Toward a convergence of psychology and metapsychology in immediate experience. *Contemporary Psychoanalysis*, *21* (1), 449-490.

Chapter 4

A Sense of Orders:
An Introduction
to the Theory of Jacques Lacan

Barbara Berger

SUMMARY. This paper provides an introduction to some of the basic concepts of the provocative French psychoanalyst Jacques Lacan. It illustrates the ways in which these concepts color the therapist's understanding of the patient as the therapist's attention is guided by the patient's expressions of thought and feeling. The response of the therapist is motivated by the interface which develops between this understanding and theoretical underpinnings. Clinical vignettes illustrating Lacan's mirror stage and his three basic orders, the Real, the Imaginary, and the Symbolic punctuate the explanations of these concepts. The paper weaves observations on the signification of language with examples of clinical interpretations. *[Article copies available from The Haworth Document Delivery Service: 1-800-342-9678. E-mail address: getinfo@haworth.com].*

Speech is the vehicle through which therapy is conducted. The dialogue between patient and therapist provides the medium through which interpretations and understanding are generated. Freud's discovery of the

Address correspondence to Barbara Berger, PhD, 30 North Michigan Avenue, Suite 909, Chicago, IL 60602.

[Haworth co-indexing entry note]: "A Sense of Orders: An Introduction to the Theory of Jacques Lacan." Berger, Barbara. Co-published simultaneously in *Journal of Analytic Social Work* (The Haworth Press, Inc.) Vol. 3, No. 2/3, 1996, pp. 83-98; and: *Narration and Therapeutic Action: The Construction of Meaning in Psychoanalytic Social Work* (ed: Jerrold R. Brandell) The Haworth Press, Inc., 1996, pp. 83-98. Single or multiple copies of this article are available from The Haworth Document Delivery Service [1-800-342-9678, 9:00 a.m. - 5:00 p.m. (EST) E-mail address: get info@haworth. com].

"talking cure" was actually the discovery of a new language, the language of the meaning of symptoms (Freud, 1895/1955, Vol. 2, p. 30). Symptoms, for Freud, are understood as symbols through which people illustrate their inner conflicts. The French psychoanalyst, Jacques Lacan, emphasized the value of Freud's discovery and urged a return to Freud with the goal of understanding the implications of Freud's greatest achievement, the discovery of the unconscious. For Lacan, the symptom is not a symbol concealing meaning, but as Ellie Ragland-Sullivan explains, "The symptom reveals 'untranslated' unconscious meaning at the surface of the body speech and action" (Ragland-Sullivan, 1986, p. 259). The signifying structure of the symptom evolves from the Lacanian concept of the symptom as the subject's interpretation of signifiers which wind together along metaphoric and metonimic pathways (Lacan & Wilden, 1968, p. 236). The study and understanding of Lacan's work offers the clinician a richer context in which to listen and comprehend within the therapeutic relationship. Lacan believed that the unconscious, because of the power of its contents, was so terrifying that it became itself subject to repression. He believed that even Freud fell prey to his own discovery and was unable to sustain the confrontation with the intolerable contents of the unconscious. As a result, Lacan said that Freud took comfort in mythical and metaphysical speculations. Freud, for example, proposed the death instinct, a destructive drive which draws what is living toward an inorganic state. Lacan interpreted this as a repudiation of the aggression that Freud felt for his own father. In this way, it was denied as Freud's own construction by ascribing biological roots. Lacan suggests that Plato's allegory of the cave whose entrance can never be reached until closing time, is a metaphor for the unconscious' insistent power of repression. In the cave of the unconscious, Lacan says, it is always closing time (Bowie, 1983, p. 119). Lacan's aim was to hold onto "the intolerable Freudian thought" (Bowie 1983, p. 120), so that "where it was, there I must come to be." Achieving the capacity to tolerate the intolerable allows an opportunity for repressed material to be returned to consciousness.

For Lacan, the unconscious has a structure which inevitably determines what an individual says and does. That structure is determined by language and, therefore, it is the linguistic structure of the unconscious that makes it accessible and objectifiable. Thus in psychoanalytic therapy, the unconscious can be heard and understood in terms of the language in the discourse between patient and therapist. Lacan's emphasis on language is one of his most innovative elaborations of classical theory.

Lacan's linguistic theory is complex, not only because of the nature of its concepts, but also because of the way in which he explains it. Unlike more traditional theorists who present a more or less clearly defined description of development, pathology, and treatment, Lacan's ideas must be interpreted from long circuitous passages in translations of his articles and seminars. It is as if the understanding of his meaning is a function, not of the comprehension of each sentence, but of the experience of Lacan's thought process. The twisting and elusive phraseology, for which Lacan is famous, forces the reader to maintain an openness to the flow of his ideas. In this way he resists the reader's impulse to assume the meaning of his thoughts prematurely. Via the necessary immersion in Lacan's speech, an osmotic process evolves by which his ideas take on form and comprehensibility. Rather than attempt to summarize ideas which do not lend themselves to reduction, this paper will offer the reader an abbreviated experience of Lacan. Theory and case material will weave together in order to explain some of his basic concepts and their clinical relevance.

Lacan's theory proposes a triad of orders he calls the Real, the Imaginary, and the Symbolic. The difficulty in understanding the triadic orders occurs because Lacan often invokes one order to help define another. They are, however, conceptual categories which, while representing different aspects of psychological life, are interrelated and, for Lacan, cover all psychic functions and activities. Each of the three has a different function, and has, thus, an independent purpose. At the same time, they are interconnected, and therefore, each relies upon the performance of the others. Lacan used the Borromean knot to illustrate the relationship of these three orders. The knot, made up of three interconnecting links, ties together in such a way that if one is cut, the others are set free (Benvenuto & Kennedy, 1986, p. 82). It is the symptom, however, which "knots" the orders. The knots develop from the signifying chains and receive their signification from the Real. It is only, then, through the Real that they can be unentangled (Lacan, 1990, p. 10).

THE REAL ORDER

The Real Order is composed of elements which exist in human beings from the earliest time, but remain outside the realm of symbolization. These are the givens, either internal or external, and may include ids, objects, instincts, desires, etc. The unconscious components and personal meanings attached to these ideas make them inaccessible to verbal symbolic expression, although they may be experienced as intensely powerful. The Real implies a hallucinatory sense of reality. In a paradoxical statement typical of Lacan, he says " . . . the feeling of real reaches its highest point in the pressing manifestation of an unreal, hallucinatory reality" (Lacan, 1988, Book 1, pp. 66-67).

The short session is a technique devised by Lacan to be employed when the Real is presented. The Lacanian short session, a session which is ended abruptly by the therapist's decision before the expected end of a therapeutic hour, may occur at any point during a session, even briefly after the opening of an hour. When a patient presents something from the Real order, the thought may appear to have vivid feelings connected to it, but the patient cannot express them in a meaningful way. Although a controversial technique, the therapist's decision to create a sudden stopping point releases the patient at a moment of turmoil in the Unconscious. This therapeutic strategy would appear to be depriving when looked at from the perspective of other therapies. It is, however, related to the essence of Lacan's approach: the effort to understand the speech of the Unconscious. The abbreviated hour provokes the frustrated unconscious into speaking by producing either a hysterical symptom or a dream. In other words, because elements of the Real can not be articulated so that they can be understood with shared meaning, the therapist must facilitate the production of an interpretable symbolic expression. Through repetitious elements of fantasy which relate to that which no one wishes to say, it becomes possible to interpret the Real in language itself. A hysterical symptom (understood as the language of the body) or a dream (the dramatic manifestation of disguised feeling) both lend themselves to interpretation within the analytic discourse. For Freud, hysteria was explained as the appearance of traumatic events pushed into consciousness in an irrational manner. For Lacan, however, there is a logic, a metaphoric rationality which gives the symptom structure. Instead of expression via appropriate speech, the response was converted into a somatic symptom which was distorted so as to keep hidden a disturbing meaning. The dream, likewise, presents its manifest content for a similar purpose. Freud theorized, and Lacan would agree, that "a symptom is a sign of, and a substitute for an instinctual satisfaction which had remained in abeyance; it is a consequence of the process of repression" (Freud 1926/1959, Vol. 20, p. 91). The belief was that the "pathology responsible for neuroses consisted of sensory experiences blocked from word association . . . " (Basch, 1981, p. 154). Nevertheless, the symptom was a sign created by the patient's linguistic knowledge and could be understood by making the patient conscious of the associational network linking a discovered traumatic event with its meaning, so that it could be articulated in speech.

TOWARD THE IMAGINARY ORDER

The Real order exists from birth and continues to be a presence in the mind throughout life. The Imaginary order, that is the realm of images, will not emerge for some months. At first, the baby's experience is one of fragmentation, as if body parts existed without connection. Lacan calls this the time of the "Fragmented I" and references to it can be illustrated by interpretation of dream symbols in the adult. Before discussing the Imaginary Order, it might be helpful to explain the Fragmented I by means of an illustration. The usefulness of insight dating from this point can be made by the example of Mr. M.

Mr. M. is a 31-year-old, hard-working, passive man who had become unemployed because the company he worked for went out of business. Even before this crisis struck, Mr. M. complained that he was unable to assert himself and was often taken advantage of at work and in social relationships. At this point, Mr. M. was feeling frustrated and unable to pursue new work. He also felt shamed by both of his very successful older brothers, who concluded that he was never able to be aggressive. The need, therefore, to become more aggressive became an important focus for him.

Mr. M.'s childhood also seemed marked by this issue. He reported that he was always alone on the playground during school recess, unable to become part of the games of others. He participated in no sports and referred to himself as a loner. Busying himself with solitary play, he tried to create the image of not caring.

Mr. M. felt very close to his father, a man whom he idealized greatly. He too was a hard-working man, but also a victim of those who took advantage of him. Ultimately, during Mr. M.'s adolescence, his father lost his manufacturing business. This changed Mr. M.'s lifestyle dramatically and was one of two traumatic events that occurred during his teen years.

The second of these traumas was his accidental discovery at age 16, that he was born prematurely with a twin brother who died shortly after birth. Mr. M. remembered being shocked and angry that no one had told him that he had a twin brother. His efforts to learn more were frustrated by his mother's refusal to talk about it. Mr. M. continues to have a great mixture of feelings around this issue. He reported the following dream.

> He was in his father's factory showroom and was aware of the presence of another man. Suddenly, the other man was outside the sliding glass doors, locked out of the showroom. Although the other man wanted to be let back in, Mr. M. said that he was pleased that he was gone and refused to help him.

At the conclusion of the session in which Mr. M. reported this dream, he turned and said as he was leaving, "Oh, I meant to ask–Do you think, I think I murdered my brother?"

This example makes clear the connection of Mr. M.'s present-day issues of shame and passivity to an early trauma dating to the time of the "Fragmented I," when body parts exist separately. His father's factory showroom, for example, symbolizes mother's womb, as if it were a separate entity. The dream also offers an example of a transformation from the Real into an interpretable presentation. The Real order experience of the twin birth can not be symbolized, but with the dream, Mr. M. illustrates some archaic sense of himself as an aggressive murderer.

The Imaginary Order

The Fragmented I of the infant evolves into a sense of unity through its reflection during what Lacan calls the "mirror phase," and the Imaginary Order emerges as a result of the 6-18 month old infant's experience in that mirror phase. It is the reflection in the mirror which gives form to the image which is "I," or that which Lacan calls the "Specular I." For Lacan, it is the function of an image to "in-form" or give form to something. Therefore, what is seen is taken in whole, without regard for object differentiation. It is the assumption of this undifferentiated reflection which forms the guidelines of the infant's development and identifications. Clearly, however, the infant's body is only one of the images which the infant sees in the mirror. Other objects seen in the reflection become confused with the visual image which is the Specular I. There is, therefore, a misidentification of the infant's body image and other. In addition, how an Other, usually mother, presents the child to the mirror will influence the ways in which the child relates to its image. Thus, identification with the image is crucial because it permanently affects the individual's experience of the self in relation to others and the external world.

An example of this concept is provided by the "earliest memory" of Ms. S. In this memory, she describes herself as a baby, not much more than one year old, being carried up a flight of stairs by her mother. As they approach the top of the staircase, Ms. S. remembers looking up into her father's angry face. He then struck out at her mother with a blow which knocked mother and baby down to the bottom of the stairs.

In the Lacanian sense, Ms. S. saw reflected in her father's face both herself and her mother. The mirror stage infant's experience, in Lacanian theory, is one in which the infant relates to mother's image as if it were her own, introjecting the desired object (Ragland-Sullivan, 1986, p. 24). It is the unified image of mother and infant which leads to a misidentification of the self and sets the stage for Ms. S.'s lifelong experience of herself with others. Lacan says this is the function of the mirror stage, " . . . to establish a relation between the organism and its reality . . . " (Lacan, 1977a, p. 4). The misidentification with the reflected image, the Specular I, also known as the specular ego is further complicated by the growing awareness of other objects also reflected in the mirror, thus leading to the evolution of the concept of I and not I. As the capacity to note that other objects have their own unity and permanence develops, the Specular I becomes the Social I and places itself, albeit with its misidentifications, within a social dialectic. That which remains and is understood as I becomes rigidly defended with the "assumption of the armour of an alienating identity, which will mark. . . . the subject's entire mental development" (Lacan, 1977a, p. 4). The Imaginary Order is, thus, the realm of the image. It grows from the infant's experience of the Specular I, and extends to the adult's experience of others and the external world. It is the Imaginary Realm which takes the dominant role any time there is a misidentification either within the subject, between subjects, or between subjects and things. For Ms. S., therefore, the confused image of herself and her mother is part of her Imaginary order and in this realm the misidentification becomes reified and rigidly defended. It is this misidentification which Lacan says forms the basis of the ego, a psychic agency evolving from the Social I, and, therefore, causing a distortion in Ms. S's experience of reality. The ego, for Lacan, is the "reified product of successive imaginary identifications" and is the "stable or would be stable seat of personal identity" (Lacan, 1951, p.12), but is characterized by paranoiac alienation. This occurs as a result of the misidentification of the subject's own self with the self in relation to others in the mirror reflection. In this case, the image is that mother has presented her to a mirror which reflected back hostility. Her ego thus (mis)identifies with the image of a woman who desires a hostile man and it is she, Ms. S., who is the object of his hostility.

In Ms. S.'s adolescence, when her mother reports her to her father for a wrongdoing, the scene is repeated. This time, however, a symbolic element is added. Ms. S. responds to a call from father inviting her to his office, without knowledge of the previous parental communication. Upon her entry, he strikes out with a blow to her face, leaving a cut on the bridge of her nose. Although Ms. S. insists that she has a permanent scar from the injury, it is not visible. This scar is part of the Imaginary, and has been endowed, unconsciously, with a special significance—it is the symbolic mark of desire, the encounter with her desired hostile man. For Lacan, desire is always for an Other, always intended to fill a lack, but always elusive. The Other can not fulfill the lack, because the desire emanates from the image in the mirror, and that image is based on distortion. The lack thus remains, demanding and insistent that it be fulfilled, becoming the lifelong pursuit for the phantom Other who might be, but cannot be, that which is desired. This example illustrates the way in which the symptom knots the orders. The Real order experience of her father, stemming from a preverbal moment in which pleasure becomes inextricably bound to pain, is linked with a scar in the Imaginary, the hysterical symptom. This, then, lends itself to interpretation through the Symbolic Order.

THE SYMBOLIC ORDER

Although the Imaginary is a separate order, it is organized and directed by the Symbolic order. The Symbolic Order is the Order of symbols, including the social and cultural. Language is part of this Order and makes organization and articulation possible. As speech is acquired, the individual submits to the preexistence of the Symbolic Order and, in psychoanalytic psychotherapy, speech becomes a function of language and a vehicle of symbolism, which is part of the culture into which the child is born. Psychoanalytic concepts "take on their full meaning only when oriented in a field of language, only when ordered in relation to the function of speech" (Lacan, 1977a, p. 39). Lacan suggests, therefore, that the analyst must be a master in the study of language because, for Lacan, language is the true center of psychoanalysis. The analyst functions as "interpreter in the discord of languages" (Muller & Richardson, 1982, p. 95).

The development of Lacanian theory in this area was heavily influenced by Ferdinand De Saussure, a French linguist in whose work a sign was defined as a representation of the interface between the bonding of thought and voice. A sign is the basic unit of semiosis and "stands for or represents something else in some way to someone" (Litowitz, 1987, p. 2). De Saussure divided the sign into two parts. He called those parts "the signifier," or that which represents with a sound-image, and "the signified," which is the concept or meaning evoked by that sound. The signifier, or sound image, could be any word and the signified is the meaning of that word, personal to an individual. For De Saussure, the signifier "table," for example, may evoke the concept of something round on a pedestal, something rectangular with four legs, smaller or larger, higher or lower. "A particular word," De Saussure acknowledged, "is like the center of a constellation: it is the point of convergence of an indefinite number of co-ordinated terms" (Litowitz, 1987, p. 9).

Lacan, however, refuted the De Saussurian semiotic notion that there was a meaning to be found at the juncture of signifier and signified. His re-formulation proposed that a signifier represents a subject for another signifier and that the signified never becomes a clear reality. In fact, it is the coalescence of signifier and signified which produces both the meaning and the reality (Lacan & Wilden, 1968, pp. 225-226). Lacan's emphasis is therefore on language, and not perception. Ragland-Sullivan poetically explains that this allows "meaning (to glide) perpetually at the surface of language in a constant 'translation' of the elements that constitute it in terms of Desire" (Ragland-Sullivan, 1988, p. 233).

Lacan used the union of analytic theory and linguistics to draw conclusions about the Symbolic Order. For him, the center of a constellation meant that one signifier was associated with another signifier, forming a signifying chain. Because language mediates all signifiers, the logical relationships of words on the surface are of little significance. In psychoanalytic work, then, it is important to recognize that the bonding of words by association represents something personally meaningful "in some way to someone" (Litowitz, 1987, p. 3). He calls the act of binding signifiers and signifieds signification. The signified, then, remains in the Imaginary Order and becomes represented in the Symbolic Order via language. Thus, "Between the enigmatic signifier . . . and the term that is substituted for it in an actual signifying chain there passes the spark that fixes in a symptom, the signification inaccessible to the conscious subject in which that symptom may be resolved–a symptom being a metaphor in which flesh or function is taken as a signifying element" (Lacan, 1977b, p. 166).

This concept is illustrated by the case of Ms. R. who entered treatment because she could not understand why she had become unnecessarily irritable and nasty with her boyfriend. In her first session, Ms. R. reported that, at age 25, in January of her sophomore year in college, she became pregnant and had an abortion. Afterward she became so depressed that she had to leave school, and for the remaining 6 months of the semester essentially confined herself to her room. During that time, she explained, she gained 24 pounds which she "carried" until recently when suddenly she "lost it." It was then, in September, when she turned 40 years old, that she entered treatment and sadly added that she'd given up the hope of ever having children.

Ms. R.'s abortion occurred about 12 weeks into the pregnancy. Those 3 months plus the 6 months she spent "in confinement," an old fashioned word often associated with the term of pregnancy, added up to nine months of normal gestation. Furthermore, conception was in the month of January and some 15 years later, in September, the ninth month, she "lost" the weight she "carried" and gave up the idea of ever having a baby. It was not difficult to connect the ninth month of her would-be pregnancy and the occasion of her 40th birthday with her symptomatic irritability. Not only was Ms. R. dealing with the conscious realization that she would never have children, but also she was unconsciously struggling with the loss of her baby from the earlier pregnancy which she'd symbolically carried for many years.

Joining linguistic and analytic concepts, Lacan explains that " . . . pathological symptoms are structured like a language . . . they have the structure of a metaphor insofar as in the symptom one signifier (with all its associations) replaces another signifier (with all its associations). The symptom is resolved when the proper word is uttered revealing the substitution" (Litowitz & Litowitz, 1983, p. 76). For Ms. R., the irritability disappeared instantly, and was replaced by a mixture of emotions which were more conscious and verbalizable, and therefore, accessible to therapy.

SYMBOLISM AND THE SIGNIFYING CHAIN

Lacan theorized that in psychoanalysis the relationship of signifies and signifiers is fixed associatively within the three orders. Signifiers are not bound to what is signified and the ways in which they become attached are not evident at first. Some signifiers, however, are provided by nature and "organize human relations in a creative way" (Lacan, 1977a, p. 20). The act of binding signifiers and signifieds is called signification and can only occur after the acquisition of language replaces representation in hallucinatory images. Thus, for Lacan, language mediates all signifiers. In psychoanalysis, words which seem on the surface to be logically equivalent, as are synonyms, are of little significance. It is more important to recognize that the bonding of words by association represents something personally meaningful "in some way to someone" (Litowitz, 1987, p. 3).

For Lacan, the term symbolic designates not only discrete elements which are signifiers, but also their systematic interrelationships. Furthermore, in Lacan's Symbolic Order, the domain of the signifier is an area of perpetual restructuring. The flow between the signifier and the signified provides access to understanding the areas of fantasy and wish fulfillment, in which the subject treats itself as an object. The relationship between signifies and signifiers develops into a signifying chain and the repetition of repressed unconscious material is due to the "insistence of the signifying chain" (Benvenuto & Kennedy, 1986, p. 92). For Lacan, until the Imaginary Order is linked to the Symbolic, a person is lost in the world of images. Lacan's Imaginary Order is "the world, the register, the dimension of images, conscious or unconscious, perceived or imagined . . . where there is a coalescence of the signifier and the signified" (Muller and

Richardson, 1982, p. 87). Repressed ideas cannot be understood until they are translated, as Freud (1915/1957, Vol. 14, p. 166) expressed it, or put into words and interpreted. This requires the uncovering and explanation of the paradigmatic relationships, or the similarities of signs at the level of signifiers, signifieds, or both. De Saussure emphasizes that paradigmatic relationships find their support in the human memory system, not in the discourse: "Their seat is in the brain; they are part of the inner storehouse that makes up the language of each speaker" (De Saussure, 1959, p. 16).

During the course of her treatment, Ms. K. reported about relationships she'd had, as well as one which she has had for most of the length of 5 years of therapy. Over time, it was observed that each relationship involved a difficulty for Ms. K. pertaining to her sexual desire. Seemingly unaware of her repetitiveness, she explained each time that her partner was just too thin to be attractive to her. In fact, she said she was "turned off" to her current boyfriend because he was so thin that the vertebrae of his back were visible and could be counted. When the therapist called the frequency of this experience to her attention and wondered about her consistent choice of thin men who were unattractive to her, Ms. K. seemed surprised, embarrassed, and unable to respond to the comment. Instead she began to recall men in her family background for whom she described a variety of feelings. Her grandfather, a tall thin man, was someone for whom she had a particular fondness. She remembered especially enjoying sitting on his lap and snuggling up to him as a child, and described him as the "backbone of the family." Perhaps, the therapist suggested, Ms. K. was in search of another man who could be strong and reliable, someone with "backbone upon whom she could count."

The signifying chain in this example ends with the signifier, "backbone." Until this linguistic term, part of the Symbolic Order, is introduced there is a coalescence of an image from the Imaginary and a repressed wish. The visible backbone of her boyfriend is linked with her grandfather. The backbone and thinness, thus, were displaced images of the desired object. A desire displaced in this way had to be defended against because of the directness of its incestuous association. This connection led to Ms. K.'s sexual inhibition. For Lacan, it is the introjection of the Symbolic which ends the dualistic process, as in this displacement of images from inside to outside. Instead, the situation becomes triangular because one is placed in relation to an other by means of a symbolic element. What is introjected is always linguistic and, therefore, always the "introjection of a relation" (Felman, 1987, p. 115).

A cognitive result of this introjective process is the ability to think consciously in purely verbal concepts. At this point, language becomes a way of symbolizing the division between the inner and outer world of a subject.

Until the linguistic intervenes, Ms. K., like the infant, is identified with the external and operates in the Imaginary Realm, the realm of images. The repetitious experience of attraction to thin men creates an "encounter with the real" and "the return, the coming back, the insistence of the signs by which we see ourselves governed by the pleasure principle" (Lacan, 1977a, p. 53). The attraction and sexual excitement are caused by the joining, the knotting, of the Real and the Imaginary with the Symbolic. It is in the repetition that Lacan discovered "nothing can be grasped, destroyed or burnt, except in a symbolic way, as one says, in effigy, in absentia" (Lacan, 1977a, p. 50). The metaphor, then, is one of presence and absence, illustrating a compulsion to focus on an absent signified object or thing, by a repeated effort to find it in the present.

REPETITION AND TRAUMA

The repeated experience of the intrusion of the past into the present leads Lacan to describe an analytic order–trauma, fixation, reproduction, transference (Lacan, 1988, Book I, p. 85). But, trauma, according to Lacan, is an ambiguous concept. From clinical evidence he concludes that there is a component of fantasy which takes place after, and is a more important aspect than the event itself. This fantasy remains part of the primary repressed. Thus, the event becomes the background for subjective experience (Lacan, 1988, Book I, p. 34). It is as if the actual event may become a reference point for the trauma, which gets established after time on the level of the Imaginary. The fantasy takes on the status of trauma because it takes a form, like the incident itself, which is shocking to the subject (Lacan, 1988, Book I, p. 191). It is, however, at some point after the event, when something else occurs, that traumatic significance is assigned. This something else strikes a chord, Lacan calls this the Pragung. A Pragung for Lacan is the occurrence of another event which resonates with the first and, thus, becomes associated with the original event (Lacan, 1988, Book I, p. 190)

The trauma's power to create a primary repression detaches something from the symbolic world of the subject, leaving it unintegrated. Yet, it becomes a central point around which symptoms develop and organize while the subject continues to operate in the Symbolic world. Once part of a primary repression the actual event becomes that which is "the unrememberable and the unforgettable" (Frank, 1969, pp. 48-77). Kingston and Cohen explain the primary repressed, according to Freud, as "some form of permanent impression on the mind which is not usable or useful" (1986, p. 338). But, for Lacan, this repressed material becomes suspended (Ragland-Sullivan, 1986, p.113), and "re-appears in something it gives rise to that presents itself in man as desire" (Lacan, 1977a, p. 286).

The primary repressed becomes the point of fixation, the central point, the nucleus of the trauma. When a Pragung occurs there is a return of the repressed, the reproduction of the Real. It is this which can appear in the transference during therapy. The previously discussed case of Mr. M. is a good illustration of the process–trauma, fixation, reproduction, transference.

Mr. M.'s dream implies that the actual event producing the trauma had to do with the premature birth of himself and his twin brother. Mr. M., at birth, exists in the realm, as we said, of the Fragmented I. He has no capacity to symbolize this experience, which becomes part of the Real Order. There is, however, a pre-existing symbolic order into which Mr. M. is born, and it is to this order which his parents and siblings belong. Symbolism will be imposed upon him later through what is said and what is not. It might be assumed, for example, that he is born to a mother who is grieving for a lost son and who is afraid to lose another. Mr. M.'s earliest life, following the traumatic birth event itself, is perhaps, characterized by a surround in which there is depression, conflict, anxiety, self doubt, resentment and fear.

Mr. M. brings to the mirror phase and, then, the Imaginary order, the fragments of his experiences, influenced by the pre-existing Symbolic Order in which he exists. When, at about age 6 months, mother, figuratively, "presents him to the mirror," the event permanently structures the way in which he will relate to the image of himself, others, and the external world. The misidentification of the self occurs by the unification of his whole body image with what else is reflected. Perhaps in the reflection he has seen mother's sadness, hurt, pain, and fear. This image of himself is, then, that of one who evokes these feelings. It may be interpreted that the precursors of Mr. M.'s passive character develop because he does not have a way to understand what he might do to create misery. Unconsciously, in the Imaginary Realm, Mr. M. has, potentially, created the fantasy that somehow he is the cause of pain and suffering. What becomes clear is that later, after traversing the oedipal phase, whether in school or on the playground, in friendships or family relationships, Mr. M. remains unassertive, tolerating the intolerable.

Mr. M., himself, entered the Symbolic Order, without access to the event, because of the primary repression, which was of the fantasy, part of the unintegrated Imaginary Realm. At the age of 16, he discovers his birth certificate. This symbol strikes the chord, it is a Pragung, which resonates with the original trauma, the primary repression. It is his identity, the sense of who he is in relation to the world which becomes threatened. He has been the inactive one, the one who accepts injury and oversight from others, but does not act. The ego is threatened with the overwhelming sense that he is an agent, an actor whose actions may be dangerous to others. He can create pain, he can even kill.

In a moment of psychological turmoil, Mr. M. was spurred to confront his parents with his discovery. While they confirmed the truth of the birth, they became upset and refused to discuss it further. The iconic sign of his birth, the birth certificate, had reawakened the "killer" in him and this time he attacked his parents. Once again, an assertive action on Mr. M.'s part had caused pain and misery. Emergency measures are needed in order for the ego to protect itself from being overwhelmed. Defenses are summoned to reinforce the threatened shield. The misidentification of the subject as victim, he who is acted upon, must be protected. Mr. M., therefore, consciously experiences his interaction with his parents as another instance in which he is deprived and must tolerate it. A consolidation occurs of his characterological passivity. It is this sequence, the Pragung–the action–the consequence– the suppression, which is reproduced periodically. This sequence will, of course, naturally reoccur during the course of an analytic psychotherapy.

It is, thus, in the context of the treatment that the Imaginary and Symbolic Orders may find connection. The Pragung, as I said, resonates with the primary repression, but remains part of the unrepressed unconscious. The trauma, the primary repression, and the Pragung are not verbalizable. They do not have signification. There is no connection between signified and signifiers. The subject, therefore, can not bring this part of himself into the Symbolic Order. Using the psycholinguistic metaphor of Bonnie Litowitz, in order to know the meaning, the "sign creator" requires a "sign reader" (Litowitz, 1987, p. 6), the therapist.

The unity of self and other in the Imaginary, the misidentification, can be replaced by a new triangular relation, that which is linguistic, in the form of a new master signifier. When the Symbolic is introjected it is the "crucial moment in which what is beginning to take place is the encroachment of language on the Imaginary of the subject" (Muller, 1988, p. 525). It is when Mr. M. asks the question, "Do you think I think I murdered my brother?" that it takes place. It is then that repressed material manifests and presents an opportunity for an access to the Real. Lacan's aim, which is to hold onto "the intolerable Freudian thought" so that "where it was, there (he) must come to be" is fulfilled, as Mr. M. begins to recognize the fictions by which he has been structured (Bowie, 1983, p.120). With the entry of Mr. M. into the Symbolic, the understanding of this structure can become part of the treatment. The trauma can, at this point, be represented in linguistic symbols. It has become accessible to interpretation and analysis.

CONCLUSION

Lacan proposed that words were the Symbolic Order which reflected the structure of the mind, the knot of the Symbolic, the Real, and the Imaginary, and the symptom. Words, once attached to certain images, become signifiers and form chains in which each signifier is associated to the ones before and after. In analytic psychotherapy, meaning can be revealed by tracing these signifying chains back toward the signifieds, the original, unconscious thoughts which are barred from speech, the signifieds. The speaking being's ultimate achievement, thus, has been the development of symbolic language. It is this achievement, Lacan theorized, that provides the discourse from which psychotherapeutic interpretations leading to insight and understanding are possible.

Lacan's emphasis on the linguistic structure of the unconscious and language as that which makes it accessible and objectifiable is a major contribution to psychoanalytic theory. He did not, however, present his work to the world in a manner which is easy to comprehend. It was presented in a number of papers, published together in Ecrits (1966) and his weekly seminars, only some of which have been translated into English. These do, however, give the student a flavor of the richness of the totality of his work.The seminars, which began in Paris in 1953, continued for many years and were Lacan's main teaching method. He never organized the totality of his work into an orderly presentation. Although it would have been a convenience to the student of Lacan, such an attempt would have countered his underlying message. To keep the mind open to the flow of ideas meant not reducing his thoughts to abbreviated explanations. A sense of order comes to the reader as one gradually comes to understand the development of Orders– Real, Imaginary, and Symbolic. In psychoanalytic psychotherapy, insight and interpretation of the unconscious become more available through the Symbolic Order, the order of speech and language.

REFERENCES

Basch, M. F. (1981). Psychoanalytic interpretation and cognitive transformation. *International Journal of Psychoanalysis*, 62, 151-75.

Benvenuto, B. & Kennedy, R. (1986). *The Works of Jacques Lacan*, New York: St. Martin's.

Bowie, M. (1983). Jacques Lacan. In J. Sturrock (Ed.), *Structuralism and Since*, Oxford: Oxford University Press.

De Saussure, F. (1959). *Course in General Linguistics* (C. Bally and A. Sechehaye, Eds.). New York: Philosophical Library.

Felman, S. (1987). *Jacques Lacan and the Adventure of Insight*. Cambridge, Mass.: Harvard University Press.

Frank, A. (1969). The Unrememberable and the Unforgettable: Passive Primal Repression. *Psychoanalytic Study of the Child*, 24: 48-77.

Freud, S. (1955). *Totem and Taboo*. In J. Strachey (Ed. and Trans.), *The Standard Edition of the Complete Psychological Works of Sigmund Freud*, Vol 13. London: Hogarth Press.

———. (1957). *The Unconscious*. S.E. 14.

———. (1955). *Beyond the Pleasure Principle*. S.E. 18.

Kingston, W. & Cohen, Jonathan. (1986). Primal Repression: Clinical and Theoretical Aspects. *International Journal of Psychoanalysis*, 67: 337-352.

Lacan, J. (1951. May 2). Some reflections on the ego. Read to the British Analytic Society.

Lacan, J. (1977a). *Ecrits*. New York: W.W. Norton.

Lacan, J. (1977b). *The Four Fundamental Concepts of Psychoanalysis*. (J.A. Miller, Ed., and Sheridan, A., Trans.). London: Hogarth Press.

Lacan, J. (1988). *The Seminar of Jacques Lacan, Book I: Freud's Papers on Technique 1953-1954*. (J.A. Miller, Ed. and Sheridan, A., Trans.). New York: W.W. Norton.

Lacan, J. (1988). *The Seminar of Jacques Lacan, Book II: The Ego in Freud's Theory and in the Technique of Psychoanalysis 1954-1955*. (J.A. Miller Ed. and Sheridan, A., Trans.). New York: W.W. Norton.

Lacan, J. (1990). *Television*. (Denis Hollier, Rosalind Krauss, Annette Michelson, Trans.). New York: W.W. Norton.

Lacan, J. & Wilden, A. (1968). *Speech and Language in Psychoanalysis*. Baltimore: Johns Hopkins University Press.

Litowitz, B. (1987, March 14). *Elements of Semiotic Theory Relevant to Psychoanalysis*. Presented at Semiotics, Psychiatry and Psychoanalysis Conference, Rush-Presbyterian St. Lukes Medical Center, Chicago, Ill.

Litowitz, B. & Litowitz, N. (1983). Development of verbal self expression. In A. Goldberg (Ed.), *The Future of Psychoanalysis*. Hillsdale, New Jersey: Analytic Press.

Muller, J. & Richardson, W. (1982). *Lacan and Language: A Reader's Guide to Ecrits*. New York: International Universities Press.

Ragland-Sullivan, E. (1986). *Jacques Lacan and the Philosophy of Psychoanalysis*. Chicago and Urbana: University of Illinois Press.

Chapter 5

Adult Re-Collections of Childhood Sexual Abuse

Janice A. Gasker

SUMMARY. A controversy exists regarding adults who come to bear memories of childhood sexual abuse. This debate in both the scientific literature and popular press has evolved into a dichotomous categorization which demands an identification of these memories as either "true" or "false." This paper will lend a theoretical foundation to the discussion, considering the phenomenon from a variety of perspectives, including: psychoanalytic, developmental and cognitive theories of psychology, folkloristic studies, and the sociology of knowledge. The goal of this consideration is to determine what can be said about "truth" in light of these memories. Implications for social work practice and research are provided. *[Article copies available from The Haworth Document Delivery Service: 1-800-342-9678. E-mail address: getinfo@haworth.com].*

Mainstream American society finds the notion of child sexual abuse, particularly incest, to be so abhorrent as to be unthinkable. (For a discussion of the development of this view, see for example Bremner, 1971; Costin, 1985; Gardner, 1992a, 1992b; and Zelizer, 1985.) In recent years, this feeling has become part of a belief that child sexual abuse may be so

Janice A. Gasker is a doctoral candidate and adjunct faculty member at the University of Pennsylvania, School of Social Work, 3701 Locust Walk, Philadelphia, PA.

[Haworth co-indexing entry note]: "Adult Re-Collections of Childhood Sexual Abuse." Gasker, Janice A. Co-published simultaneously in *Journal of Analytic Social Work* (The Haworth Press, Inc.) Vol. 3, No. 2/3, 1996, pp. 99-111; and: *Narration and Therapeutic Action: The Construction of Meaning in Psychoanalytic Social Work* (ed: Jerrold R. Brandell) The Haworth Press, Inc., 1996, pp. 99-111. Single or multiple copies of this article are available from The Haworth Document Delivery Service [1-800-342-9678, 9:00 a.m. - 5:00 p.m. (EST) E-mail address: get info@haworth.com].

unthinkable as to be repressed for years, even decades, and then finally recalled in adulthood, often as part of a therapeutic process aimed at seeking out the causes of current psychosocial disturbances (Goldstein & Farmer, 1992, 1993; Lawrence 1993; Tavris, 1993).

A controversy currently rages around this issue among mental health professionals. The issue at hand is whether brand-new memories of old trauma may be historically accurate recollections of real events or simply re-collections; that is, images that are pieced together which come to be part of our self-constructed life stories. The relationship between repressed memory and adult re-collections of childhood sexual abuse has been framed as a true-or-false debate by both the popular and scientific media. On one hand, adults who come to bear memories of childhood sexual abuse are thought to be the helpless victims of incest who are only further damaged by mental health professionals and others who doubt the credibility of their reports (Berliner, 1993; Freyd, 1993; Lawrence, 1993; Maltz, 1990; and Maltz & Holman, 1987). It is felt that the process of questioning reporters' credibility may not only harm the individual but may result in a return to the days when women and children who reported sexual mistreatment were disbelieved as a matter of course.

The other side of the argument also sees the reporters as victims–not of sexual abuse, but of misguided, overzealous therapists who in their zeal to ferret out memories of childhood trauma succeed only in suggesting it (see, for example, Ganaway, 1993; Gardner, 1992b; Goldstein & Farmer, 1992; Lief, 1993; Perry, 1993). Therapists are viewed as implanting memories which are revisited in the therapeutic process in excruciating detail, leaving the bearer of the memories with the same degree of trauma as if the actual abuse had occurred.

While proponents of both views continue the debate, people are living in anguish. The context of the social work profession, with its traditional ties to psychoanalytic theory and child protection activity, places the profession in a position to shed light on this issue from a broad theoretical perspective.

This paper will draw on reports from the scientific literature, the popular press, and the statements of affected persons to consider the phenomenon from a variety of theoretical perspectives. An analysis of what may be considered "truth" regarding these memories will follow, along with a discussion of what all this may mean for the field of social work.

TRAUMA, MEMORY AND RE-COLLECTIONS

The controversy regarding adults who come to bear memories of childhood abuse centers around fundamental beliefs about the nature of the human memory of experience. Memory, particularly as is relates to traumatic events, has long been the focus of scientific inquiry.

Psychoanalytic Theory

Drive theory. The belief that traumatic memories are accurate representations of objective reality which may exist unchanged outside of consciousness is as old as the systematic study of psychiatry. Freud's earliest work, that of seduction theory, in which he postulated that emotional disturbance is the result of repressed childhood trauma, had this concept at its foundation. Freud later moved from seduction theory to drive theory, which holds that statements regarding childhood sexual abuse may be the result of id-driven fantasy. Due to this change in focus from memories of trauma to memories of fantasy, it is common for Freud to be blamed for the decades-long disbelief of women and children who reported sexual mistreatment (Masson, 1984).

Regardless of whether drive theory may or may not be antithetical to the concept that child sexual abuse exists, Freud's real contribution to the question of the accuracy of traumatic memories lies in his work on childhood and concealing memories. In his essay on this topic, written in 1899, Freud suggested that while childhood memories might be inaccurate due to the child's perceptions of actual traumatic life events, the accurate memory may be intact. That is, accurate memories may be stored and hidden by concealing, or screen, memories. These memories are viewed as historically accurate and retrievable in psychoanalysis (Freud, 1899).

Freud used convincing case studies as well as introspective autobiographical accounts to support his views. This work supports the generalized acceptance of traumatic memories as historically accurate, particularly those which have grown out of the helping process. While many of Freud's ideas have been subjected to modern empirical study, his notions about memory have not been systematically evaluated (Fisher & Greenberg, 1985).

Dissociation. Freud was not the first to address the subject of traumatic event memory. As early as 1886, Pierre Janet documented the opinion, based on case studies, that traumatic event memory could exist intact, outside of consciousness (Van der Kolk & Van der Hart, 1991). While the concepts of dissociation and repression are frequently used interchangeably, the ideas are rooted in the work of Janet on dissociation. As a defense mechanism, the concept of dissociation refers specifically to unconscious material stored in such a way as to render other material inaccessible. While Freud was unclear as to how repressed material might be stored out of consciousness, Janet viewed dissociated material as stored in a specific way along with a specific affect. He postulated that the affective content of the dissociated material determines the accessibility of the information (Spiegel, 1990). One case study which supported this theory involved a woman who did not consciously remember her mother's death but acted out the traumatic incident repeatedly and with unvarying detail when under stress (Van der Kolk & Van der Hart, 1991).

Van der Kolk and Van der Hart (1991) have postulated that animal research revealing physiological changes under conditions of stress support Janet's original theory and have concluded that a subject may maintain a traumatic memory outside of consciousness, but re-experience it when in another environmentally or emotionally similar situation. This model describes the processing of trauma as a dissociation from consciousness, a widely-accepted theory employed in the treatment of a wide range of trauma victims and those who suffer from the set of symptoms known as post traumatic stress disorder (Brom, Kleber, & Witzum, 1992; Classen, Koopman, & Spiegel, 1993; Kluft, 1992; Young, 1992).

The work of Janet and those who followed him–most particularly Freud, began a new perspective on the therapeutic use of memory. Traumatic childhood memories came to be viewed as the cause of many emotional disturbances. For this reason, the memories had to be sought out. Such techniques as hypnosis, dream analysis, and free association were developed as part of psychoanalysis, specifically for shedding light on memories hidden in the unconscious (Fisher & Greenberg, 1985).

A comprehensive review of the literature (Tillman, Nash & Lerner, in press) has suggested that most contemporary theories regarding trauma and its treatment have adopted similar models, in which a goal of treatment is the uncovering of traumatic memories. It should be noted that theories which explain information processing are generally cognitive in their orientation; however, the majority of those regarding trauma assume the psychoanalytic constructs of repression and dissociation (e.g., Burgess & Hartman, 1988).

Traditional psychoanalytic theory, then, suggests that memory of traumatic events may be historically accurate. The trauma may be dissociated or repressed when it occurs and retrieved later in life–particularly while undergoing psychoanalysis. This way of thinking appears to be the foundation for the polarization of the debate regarding the historical accuracy of adult re-collection of childhood sexual abuse.

However, this view is an over-simplification. Janet provided the foundation for the concept of the dissociation of traumatic memory, but he also wrote: "It is not necessary that the carriage wheel should really have passed over the patient; it is enough if he has the idea that the wheel passed over his legs" (Janet, 1907, p. 324). Likewise, dissociation in Sullivan's object-relations theory was a functionally distinct subset of personality created as a defense against anxiety created by general themes–not specific events–in early relationships (Newman, 1990). Finally, Freud explored the idea that particular childhood memories may be related in a symbolic fashion during the psychoanalytic process, making the narrative choices in relating them grist for the analytic mill:

> . . . the so-called earliest childhood recollections are not true memory traces but later elaborations of the same, elaborations which might have been subjected to the influences of many later psychic forces. (Freud, 1899, p. 65)

Relating memories in a certain way for a certain purpose in the psychoanalytic setting has captured the attention of Spence (1982). As a result, he has conceptualized *narrative truth* as the construction of meaning and memory in the therapeutic interaction. Spence wrote that memory is a construction which is formulated and re-formulated over time:

> . . . the criterion we use to decide when a certain experience has been captured to our satisfaction . . . depends on continuity and closure and the extent to which the fit of the pieces takes on an aesthetic finality. (p. 31)

Cognitive Psychological Theory

Cognitive psychological theory has suggested a perspective on adult re-collections of childhood sexual abuse which has been characterized as being in opposition to that proposed by psychoanalytic theory. In fact, there appear to be more similarities than differences.

From this perspective, autobiographical memory, held as belief, is the creation of a person in concert with the social milieu. There is both empirical and anecdotal support in the field of cognitive psychology for concluding that the potential exists for the development of images perceived to be memories which do not correspond to historical events (Furer, 1993; Gavigan-Reno, 1993; Goldstein & Farmer, 1993; Loftus & Davies, 1984; Loftus & Fathi, 1985; Loftus & Greene, 1980; Loftus & Loftus, 1980).

Bartlett's (1932) classic work on memory is an example. One of the first comprehensive works in the field of cognitive science, the book is based on laboratory studies conducted with large numbers of educated adults in war-time London. Bartlett asked his subjects to perform a number of tasks related to perception, imagery and recall. His findings suggested that as events occur, a static "trace" is not created in the brain. Rather, he suggested that the past seems to operate as an organized mass. Elaborating on the then-new concept of "schema," Bartlett called this type of organization an *active* organization of past experiences in which present and past are combined and shuffled to meet current needs. To explain this narrative process, he suggested that persons follow a course of memory development related to their surrounding and their self-images: "This and this and this must have occurred, in order that my present state should be what it is" (p. 202).

The work of Elizabeth Loftus is most often cited as an example of an hypothesis-testing method of looking at the way in which memory of events, particularly traumatic ones, is an individual and social production. Loftus has coined the phrase "misinformation effect" and has demonstrated in hundreds of experiments the effect of suggestion on the accuracy of memory. Recently, she demonstrated the potential for implanting a traumatic memory (of being lost in a mall as a child). The memory of being lost in a mall as a child came to be believed by both adolescent and adult subjects based on one manipulative suggestion by a researcher and the corroboration of a family member (Loftus, 1993). While studies such as this do not demonstrate that new memories of past childhood sexual abuse are false, they do lend support to the notion that some memories are the product of both individual and social factors. While these may be perceived as personal experiences, they may not correspond to historical events.

At a recent False Memory Syndrome Conference, Campbell Perry, a cognitively-oriented professor of psychiatry at Concordia University, made note of a famous occurrence of the implantation of a memory: the "kidnapping" of Jean Piaget. Perry said:

> . . . We have the testament of Jean Piaget, the noted Swiss psychologist, of an early memory of about age two of an attempt to kidnap him in his pram. Almost 13 years later when he was 15, his former nanny wrote a letter to his parents saying that she had contrived the whole incident and returned the watch she had received for her presumed valor on that occasion. But what's interesting is that Piaget writes, years later, that he can still visualize the whole set of events, even though he knows that they are wrong and that they didn't happen and the whole thing was fabricated by the nanny and that it was probably the result of his parents talking about it over the years . . . . (1993)

Current literature in cognitive science clearly supports the potential for the development of historically inaccurate memories. Therapeutic implications which have grown from this perspective include the use of psycho-educational and present-oriented techniques geared toward altering dysfunctional beliefs (e.g., Jehu, Klassen & Gazan, 1985).

At the same time, cognitive psychology does not completely rule out the potential for the sudden appearance of historically accurate memories as suggested by psychoanalytic theory. Most interventions, even those based on cognitive theory, with persons identified as sexual abuse survivors include a focus on memories of the traumatic event (Haugaard & Reppucci, 1988). The degree of focus varies, as does the assumption that these memories are historically accurate. What is clear is the division between those who choose to question the validity of such memories and those who choose not to question.

Folkloristic Studies

In an effort to get beyond this division, the field of folklore is surveyed here regarding adult re-collections of childhood sexual abuse. This area of inquiry provides a different perspective. Interestingly, however, this perspective also yields an apparently polarized view.

Urban myths. On one hand, the study of folklore may view beliefs of such phenomena as satanic ritual abuse (often linked to adult re-collections of childhood sexual abuse) as socially-produced urban myths. Victors (1993) has studied beliefs regarding incidences and experiences of satanic ritual abuse. In a comprehensive study of regions in which such reports were openly discussed and reported in local newspapers, he concluded that there was no historically accurate basis for the beliefs. In other words, he could find no evidence that satanic cults were operating in the area. He tied the beliefs of ritual abuse to general societal unrest and suggested that while such beliefs may be held by individuals (and, consequently believed to be personal experiences) they were in fact socially produced. No individual's experience of satanic ritual abuse was necessary to create a community's belief in it. Similar interpretations have been made regarding beliefs in supernatural experiences.

Regarding adult re-collection of childhood sexual abuse, it has been suggested that satanic ritual abuse myths, "new age" thought, feminism, "recovery" therapy and media influence have all influenced the development of such beliefs (Goldstein & Farmer, 1992). The perspective of the urban myth has the benefit of highlighting the powerful impact of the community. This folkloristic study suggests that consideration of social forces is a necessary component of any systematic inquiry into the phenomenon of adult re-collections of childhood sexual abuse. An exclusive focus, however, on the role played by social factors in the exploration of this phenomenon could result in a suppression of the voice of the bearers of memories and a misrepresentation of their individual experiences.

Community interpretation of common experiences. The folkloristic perspective may also study the stories people tell about themselves based on reports of individual experience. Hufford (1982, 1993) has developed an experiential theory from such a perspective.

An empirically-grounded theory of beliefs developed to explain beliefs and corresponding legends about supernatural events, experiential theory explores beliefs as they are held by individuals about themselves in a manner which to the greatest extent possible respects their integrity as reporters. This conceptualization demands the exploration of the possibility of an historically accurate traumatic experience which supports beliefs about any type of trauma experience. Therefore, it is individual perceptions which are of interest; there is an avoidance of any attempts to determine the historical accuracy or inaccuracy of the beliefs.

Experiential theory highlights the possibility that a trauma of some type is the foundation for the development of a belief that childhood sexual abuse has occurred. This consideration of perceived experiences also must be part of any inquiry into the truth of adult re-collections of childhood sexual abuse.

Sociology of Knowledge

The beginnings of a reconciliation between perspectives which view beliefs as socially-produced against those which view beliefs as produced individually may be found in the study of the sociology of knowledge. Berger and Luckmann's treatment of the sociology of knowledge in their treatise on the social construction of reality (1967) provides a vehicle for making sense of knowledge as socially constructed, but with a firm base in the experience of the individual.

This analysis of the process of the construction of belief suggests a dynamic society of individuals interacting and shaping each others' beliefs. It includes consideration of phenomena which seem to be independent of one's apprehension. This perception leads to the intersubjective nature of reality in which persons interact and communicate to negotiate what is real. For example, if reality becomes problematic as perceived, the perceiver seeks to incorporate it through interaction with others. Thus, persons together communicate and evolve a determination of what is real, what experiences have occurred, and what these mean to our lives. For this theory, which has Marxism (in its identification of society as an important determinant of consciousness), historicism (in its perspective that historical situations must be viewed in their contexts), and the writings of

Nietzsche (for his thoughts on the social function of deception and self-deception) as intellectual antecedents, language objectifies experience. Recent findings of researchers in the field of sociolinguistics indicate that communication is a collaborative phenomenon and consequently support this theory (Kendon, 1990).

CONCLUSION:
TRUTH AS IMPROVISATION

Truth is an elusive concept at all times. It is most particularly so in light of the phenomenon of adult re-collections of childhood sexual abuse. For psychoanalytic theory, traumatic memories are perhaps historically accurate, but need to be interpreted in the context of the telling. Cognitive psychology clearly demonstrates the potential for the development of very real memories which are not historically accurate, but which demonstrate the product of dynamic mental processes. Folklore studies point simultaneously to the importance of individual and collective experience to the development of memory and belief. The sociology of knowledge suggests that what is true is based in individual perceptions as those are interpreted in a dynamic, meaning-making society.

Interaction is the common thread. The concept of collaborative meaning-making holds promise for the question of what is truth in light of adult re-collections of sexual abuse. The perspective that communication is a collaborative phenomenon has been explored by Fogel (1993) in the field of developmental psychology. Ideas about memory and interactional communication have lead to the concept of *embodied cognition*. Embodied cognition refers to cognitive aspects of relationships. Based on empirically-grounded assertions regarding developmental changes in communication, the concept of embodied cognition acknowledges that a central feature of relationships is the creation of information through perception and cognition. Cognition is conceptualized as:

> . . . embodied and relational, a reflection of our participation in a dynamic perception-action system, not a record of objective or represented contents of 'reality.' (Fogel, 1993, p. 120)

This view of cognition is useful in the context of the exploration of truth in adult re-collections of childhood sexual abuse for several reasons. It recognizes the role of both the individual perceptual and collective experience in creating memory. In this way, neither the social influence nor the individual voice is suppressed. In addition, the function of any re-collection becomes its own truth in the moment. In other words, the truth of a memory has to do with its purpose in the present context. Truth is negotiated between the individual holding the perception of trauma and any individuals who are playing the active role of listener in the interaction.

This is not to suggest viewing the phenomenon of adult re-collections of childhood sexual abuse under the diffuse light of absolute relativism. It is to suggest that the concepts of collaborative meaning-making and constructivism be applied to the discussion. Bruner (1990) has melded the fields of cognitive science and literary analysis to suggest that a perspective which includes consideration of collaborative meaning-making and constructivism of memory need not result in inescapable relativism:

> Constructivism's basic claim is simply that knowledge is "right" or "wrong" in light of the perspective we have chosen to assume. Rights and wrongs of this kind—however well we can test them—do not sum to absolute truths and falsities. The best we can hope for is that we be aware of our own perspective and those of others when we make our claims of "rightness" and "wrongness." (p. 25)

The view of re-collection as narrative with a specific meaning-making purpose has relevance for social work inquiry into adult re-collections of childhood sexual abuse in a number of ways. First, it is a way of allowing structured inquiry without suppressing client perceptions in favor of historical events. Second, it is consistent with social work values in that it views memory holders as active agents in the creation of their own life stories, potentially more consciously powerful social agents in the creation of the shared development of truths. Finally, it recognizes the inherent impact of re-collection on the here-and-now experience of clients: "Memories are active experiences in the present and they mean something different each time they are remembered" (Fogel, 1993, p. 127). This suggests the potential power of the use of re-collection in the therapeutic process as a powerful, dynamic force which shapes emotions and behaviors.

Ultimately, the truth is in the telling and its social context. While this perspective does not begin to answer the question of the historical accuracy of re-collections, it does free the social worker from any of the prevalent debates. In sum, the role of re-collection in the therapeutic process is one of constructive meaning-making. Considered in this light, re-collection becomes a vehicle for both client and therapist to be empowered as co-creators of the life narrative. At that point, client and therapist together can harness the power of re-collections toward therapeutic progress.

BIBLIOGRAPHY

Bartlett, F.C. (1932). *Remembering: A study in experimental and social psychology*. London: Cambridge University Press.

Berger, P., & Luckmann, T. (1967). *The social construction of reality: A treatise in the sociology of knowledge*. New York: Anchor Books.

Berliner, L. (1993). *Treatment of sexual abuse survivors*. Paper presented at False Memory Syndrome Foundation Conference, Valley Forge, PA. April 16.

Bremner, R. (Ed.). (1971). *Children and youth in America: A documentary history*. Cambridge, MA: Harvard University Press.

Brom, D., Kleber, R., & Witzum, E. (1992). The prevalence of posttraumatic psychopathology in the general and the clinical population. *Journal of Psychiatry-Related Science, 28*(4), 53-63.

Bruner, J. (1990). *Acts of meaning*. Cambridge: Harvard University Press.

Burgess, A., & Hartman, C. (1988). Information processing of trauma: Case application of a model. *Journal of Interpersonal Violence, 3*, 443-457.

Classen, C., Koopman, C., & Spiegel, D. (1993). Trauma and dissociation. *Bulletin of the Menninger Clinic, 57*, 178-194.

Costin, L. (1985). The historical context of child welfare. In J. Laird & A. Hartman, (Eds.), *A handbook of child welfare: Context, knowledge and practice* (pp. 154-175). New York: The Free Press.

Fisher, S., & Greenberg, R. (1985). *The scientific credibility of Freud's theories and therapy*. New York: Columbia University Press.

Fogel, A. (1993). *Developing through relationships*. Chicago: University of Chicago Press.

Freud, S. (1899). Childhood and concealing memories. In A.A. Brill (Ed.) (1938), *The basic writings of Sigmund Freud* (pp. 62-68). New York: The Modern Library.

Freyd, J. (1993). *Theoretical and personal perspectives on the delayed memory debate*. Paper presented at the Center for Mental Health at Foote Hospital's Continuing Education Conference: Controversies Around Recovered Memories of Incest and Ritualistic Abuse, Ann Arbor, MI. August 23.

Furer, J. (1993). *A retractor's story*. Oral presentation made at the False Memory Syndrome Foundation Conference, Valley Forge, PA. April 16.

Ganaway, G. (1993). *Transference in memory development*. Paper presented at False Memory Syndrome Foundation Conference, Valley Forge, PA. April 16.

Gardner, R. (1992a). *Sex abuse hysteria: Salem witch trials revisited*. Cresskill, NJ: Creative Therapeutics.

Gardner, R. (1992b). *True and false accusations of child sexual abuse*. Cresskill, NJ: Creative Therapeutics.

Gavigan-Reno, M. (1993). *A retractor's story*. Oral presentation made at the False Memory Syndrome Foundation Conference, Valley Forge, PA. April 16.

Goldstein, E., & Farmer, K. (1992). *Confabulations: Creating false memories, destroying families*. Boca Raton, FL: Social Issues Resources Series.

Goldstein, E., & Farmer, K. (1993). *True stories of false memories*. Boca Raton, FL: Social Issues Resources Series.

Haugaard, J., & Reppucci, N.D. (1988). *The sexual abuse of children.* San Francisco: Jossey-Bass.

Hufford, D. (1982). *The terror that comes in the night: An experience-centered study of supernatural assault traditions.* Philadelphia: University of Pennsylvania Press.

Hufford, D. (1993). *Beings without bodies.* Unpublished manuscript, University of Pennsylvania, Philadelphia.

Janet, P. (1907). *The major symptoms of hysteria.* New York: Hafner Publishing.

Jehu, D., Klassen, C., & Gazan, M. (1985). Cognitive restructuring of distorted beliefs associated with childhood sexual abuse. *Journal of Social Work and Human Sexuality, 4*(1), 49-69.

Kendon, A. (1990). *Conducting interaction: Patterns of behavior in focused encounters.* New York: Cambridge University Press.

Kluft, R. (1992). The use of hypnosis with dissociative disorders. *Psychiatric Medicine, 10*(4), 31-46.

Lawrence, L. (1993). Backlash: A look at the abuse-related amnesia and delayed memory controversy. *Moving Forward: A Newsjournal for Survivors of Sexual Child Abuse and Those Who Care for Them, 2*(4), 1.

Lief, H. (1993). Psychiatry's challenge: Defining an appropriate therapeutic role when child abuse is suspected. *Psychiatric News,* August 21.

Loftus, E. (1993). *Memory distortion.* Paper presented at the meeting of the False Memory Syndrome Foundation, Valley Forge, PA. April 16.

Loftus, E., & Davies, G. (1984). Distortions in the memory of children. *Journal of Social Issues, 40*(2), 51-67.

Loftus, E., & Fathi, D. (1985). Retrieving multiple autobiographical memories. *Social Cognition, 3,* 280-295.

Loftus, E., & Greene, E. (1980). Warning: Even memory for faces may be contagious. *Law and Human Behavior, 4,* 323-334.

Loftus, E., & Loftus, G. (1980). On the permanence of stored information in the human brain. *American Psychologist, 35,* 409-420.

Maltz, W. (1990). Adult survivors of incest: How to help them overcome the trauma. *Medical Aspects of Human Sexuality, 12,* 42-47.

Maltz, W., & Holman, B. (1987). *Incest and sexuality: A guide to understanding and healing.* Lexington, MA: Lexington Books.

Masson, J. (1984). *The assault on truth.* New York: Penguin Books.

Newman, K. (1990). Harry Stack Sullivan. In H.A. Bacal & K. M. Newman, (Eds.), *Theories of object relations: Bridges to self psychology,* pp. 28-52. New York: Columbia University Press.

Perry, C. (1993). *Hypnotic enhancement of memory.* Paper presented at the meeting of the False Memory Syndrome Foundation, Valley Forge, PA. April 16.

Spence, D. (1982). *Narrative truth and historical truth: Meaning and interpretation in psychoanalysis.* New York: W.W. Norton.

Spiegel, D. (1990). Hypnosis, dissociation and trauma. In J. L. Singer (Ed.), *Repression and dissociation: Implications for personality theory, psychopathology, and health,* pp. 121-142. Chicago: University of Chicago Press.

Tavris, C. (1993). Beware the incest-survivor machine. *New York Times*, January 3. Reprinted in *False Memory Syndrome Foundation Newsletter*, pp. 13-15. January 8.

Tillman, J.G., Nash, M.R., & Lerner, P.M. (in press). Does trauma cause dissociative pathology? In S.J. Lynn (Ed.), *Dissociation: Clinical, theoretical and research perspectives* (pp. 90-109). Washington, DC: American Psychological Press.

Van der Kolk, B., & Van der Hart, O. (1991). The intrusive past: The flexibility of memory and the engraving of trauma. *American Imago, 48*, 425-454.

Victors, J. (1993). *Satanic panic: The creation of a contemporary legend*. Chicago: Open Court.

Young, L. (1992). Sexual abuse and the problem of embodiment. *Child Abuse and Neglect, 16*(1), 89-100.

Zelizer, V. (1985). *Pricing the priceless child: The changing social value of children*. New York: Basic Books.

Chapter 6

Narrative Re-Telling in Clinical Treatment: A Single Case Study

Catherine H. Nye

SUMMARY. This study describes the telling and re-telling of one narrative across the course of a two and one half year psychoanalysis. Changes in the structure and content of the story are documented in order to describe the dynamic narrative process through which the story is told and retold, and to understand how the repeated tellings function in the treatment. *[Article copies available from The Haworth Document Delivery Service: 1-800-342-9678. E-mail address: getinfo@ haworth.com].*

There is now in clinical treatment widespread interest in narrative. What is meant by "narrative," however, varies widely. The study of narrative encompasses a range of topics from the psychoanalytic narrative and the hermeneutic process through which it is constructed, to the linguistic structure of narrative as discourse. This paper will attempt to map a very

---

Catherine H. Nye, PhD, is a faculty member at the Smith College School for Social Work, Northampton, MA.

Special thanks are due to Sherwood Waldron, President of the Psychoanalytic Research Consortium.

Funding for and assistance with this research was provided by the Clinical Research Institute, Smith College School for Social Work, and the Psychoanalytic Research Consortium, Inc.

[Haworth co-indexing entry note]: "Narrative Re-Telling in Clinical Treatment: A Single Case Study." Nye, Catherine H. Co-published simultaneously in *Journal of Analytic Social Work* (The Haworth Press, Inc.) Vol. 3, No. 2/3, 1996, pp. 113-136; and: *Narration and Therapeutic Action: The Construction of Meaning in Psychoanalytic Social Work* (ed: Jerrold R. Brandell) The Haworth Press, Inc., 1996, pp. 113-136. Single or multiple copies of this article are available from The Haworth Document Delivery Service [1-800-342-9678, 9:00 a.m. - 5:00 p.m. (EST) E-mail address: get info@ haworth.com].

113

circumscribed area of this narrative terrain: client stories of personal experience which are told repeatedly in treatment.

As clinicians, we are aware that in treatment our clients revisit certain seminal lived experiences and events. Stories about these events and experiences are told and retold, and reference to them is made repeatedly across the course of treatment. These events and experiences may also be revisited through transference and countertransference and through symptom formation. The stories the client tells and retells about these experiences and events provide one of our basic sources of clinical data. It is from our work with the client around these stories, in interaction with other available clinical data and our theoretical formulations, that a shared understanding of the client's problems, dynamics, and development emerges. This paper will explore the repeated tellings of one such client story in order to describe the structure and content of the dynamic narrative process through which the story is told and retold, and to understand how these repeated tellings function in the treatment.

The repeated telling of narratives of personal experience by children and adults has been studied in treatment and other contexts. Children tell and retell stories when their content involves difficult, problematic material. They may also reenact such material in repetitive play. While retelling can provide an opportunity for reworking and resolving, the repetition may also heighten the child's anxiety about the material (Terr, 1988). Though many of the studies of children's narrative retellings have focused on retelling stories of traumatic experience (see, for example, Terr, 1981; Herman & Schatzow, 1987), children may also use the repeated telling of other types of narratives to master difficult content (Miller, 1993).

Adults, like children, can use the repeated telling of narratives of personal experience to resolve and master difficult aspects of that experience. Adult retelling of trauma narratives, both in (Agger & Jensen, 1990; Boudwyns, Meyer, Woods, Harrison & McCranie, 1990; Cienfuegos & Monelli, 1983) and out (Nye, 1993) of treatment, has been widely studied. In the treatment of adult victims of trauma, telling and retelling narratives of traumatic experience is an essential element of treatment (Herman, 1992). Less, however, is known about the retelling of stories about other types of events and experiences. This paper, by exploring one client's repeated tellings of a story about a childhood experience, will attempt to increase our understanding of how adults retell stories of non-traumatic experience in treatment, and how these repeated tellings function in clinical process.

The client in this case, Anna, is a working-class woman in her thirties, married with two children, who is not employed outside her home. She enters treatment because she sometimes has phobic symptoms of vomiting and diarrhea when she goes out. As a result of the treatment, these symptoms are reduced. The treatment was a 2 1/2 year analysis (four sessions per week) by a senior analyst. The client paid a reduced fee in exchange for allowing the sessions to be taped, transcribed, and used for research.

Over the course of her treatment, Anna tells many stories. One that she returns to again and again is about her experience of being taken to school for the first time by her father. The "single case" referred to in the title of this paper is not, then, the clinical case itself, but rather this story, which the client tells and retells. I elected to follow this particular story somewhat by chance; it was the only story that was retold in a sample set of ten sessions randomly selected for a previous study using this data (Nye, 1994). Locating multiple tellings of this story across the 324 sessions of the treatment was made possible by computer technology. (The Psychoanalytic Research Consortium, funded in part by a grant from the Clinical Research Institute, Smith College School for Social Work, entered the transcripts on computer discs, making it possible to search the data and retrieve the relevant stories.) Despite repeated searches of the data it is, of course, possible that there are additional tellings that have not been located.

The first task of this paper is to describe the dynamic narrative process through which Anna tells and retells this one story over the course of her treatment. Even at first reading, it is clear that Anna's narrative is not static, it changes with retelling. Microanalysis of this data should make it possible to document the dynamic nature of narrative process in this clinical treatment. In the process of telling, new awareness of the experience itself and of its meanings emerges. Anna's understanding and awareness of this event change with, and are reflected in, her changing story. In this analysis, attention will be paid to both the structure of the process and to changing narrative content.

THE FIRST TELLING: SESSION SIX

Anna's first account of this experience occurs during the sixth session, in the second week of her treatment. She is telling her analyst about her sense that her mother was often absent during her childhood. She says:

> We weren't together very often. . . . I remember being by my grandmother's so much. You know, I very seldom remember being home, uh-

and then, for the first time, she describes the event, using it as a specific example to illustrate the point she is making to the analyst.

> I know I was like, uh, five going on six when I started first grade and my mother didn't take me, my father walked me and, uh, the same with like, uh–I remember my father doing a lot of things and not my mother. He took me to the first grade the first few times not my mother.

Anna then goes on to describe a series of occasions when her father did things for or with her which her mother did not.

This first account does not constitute a fully developed narrative. It lacks a temporal juncture (Labov & Waletsky, 1967), a sequence of events–first this happened and then that happened. It is a simple description of one event, one moment in time. Like the events in a narrative, however, this single event, "when I started first grade my father walked me," is evaluated. The clause "my mother didn't take me" stands as an evaluative comment and conveys the meaning the event had for Anna. The immediate repetition of these two clauses, "He took me to the first grade the first few times not my mother," serves to emphasize this contrast. What is important to Anna is not only what her father did, but what her mother failed to do. As we follow the narrative process we will find these two clauses repeated, and the themes they represent elaborated, over the course of the treatment.

STRUCTURAL ASPECTS OF NARRATIVE PROCESS

Over the 324 sessions of the treatment, Anna narrates this story four times, in sessions 41, 58, 117, and 173. She refers to the event an additional nine times (in sessions 17, 44, 52, 81, 152, 159, 252, 269, and 305) for a total of fifteen occurrences. Her narration and discussion of this event are distributed over the course of the treatment, but focus on it is most intense during the first eighteen months (see Figure 1). During the first six months of treatment, for example, she narrates the event twice (in sessions 41 and 58) and mentions it four additional times (in sessions 6, 17, 44, and 52). During the second six months of treatment she narrates it once, in session 117 and refers to it in one other session (81). In the third six-month period Anna tells her story in narrative form for the final time, in session 173, and mentions it in two other sessions (152 and 159). In the fourth six-month period, between eighteen months and two years of treatment, Anna men-

FIGURE 1

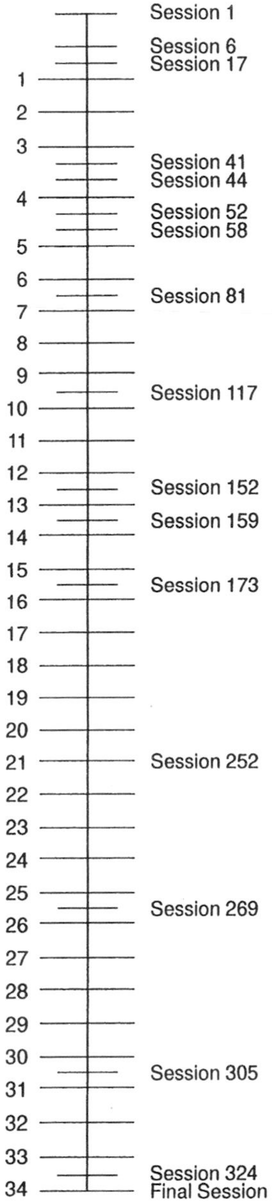

Session 1
Session 6
Session 17
1
2
3
Session 41
Session 44
4
Session 52
Session 58
5
6
7 Session 81
8
9
10 Session 117
11
12
13 Session 152
14 Session 159
15
16 Session 173
17
18
19
20
21 Session 252
22
23
24
25
26 Session 269
27
28
29
30
31 Session 305
32
33
34 Session 324
Final Session

Months in Treatment
0 - 34

tions this event only once, in session 252. In the six months of treatment from 2 to 2 1/2 years Anna mentions the event once, in session 269, and in the final four months to termination mentions it again in session 305. This distribution of occurrences suggests that work around this story was most intense during the first eighteen months of treatment, though Anna, and her analyst, continue to refer back to it. She mentions it for the last time three months before termination.

The length of Anna's narratives and comments about this event vary in length from two lines (in session 22) to twenty-two lines (in session 252). Reference to the event is generally initiated by Anna, though in session 252 it is the analyst who refers to it.

CONTENT OF NARRATIVE PROCESS

As we shift our focus from the structure of the narrative process to its changing content over multiple retellings, we can trace the emergence and development of two central themes. These themes are represented by the clauses "my father took me" and "my mother didn't take me." These phrases are repeated by Anna, in only slightly varying form, across four tellings (in sessions 6, 41, 44, and 52) and are echoed by the analyst in sessions 159 and 252. In their repetition these phrases acquire force and power; they emerge as the leitmotif of the narrative. Their meaning is elaborated, becomes more complex, and is enriched with each retelling.

Session 17

Three weeks after she first mentions the event in session 6, Anna returns to it in session 17. In this session she is working actively to understand her symptom. She reviews various childhood experiences, trying to discover some link with her present difficulties–her fear and physical symptoms of vomiting and diarrhea when she goes out, particularly with her husband. She proposes quite speculatively:

> I got the feeling maybe now it's tied in with my mother somewhere– maybe I was close to her when I was little and to go to first grade– my father taking me–just was separation from her and now that I'm a mother like her and all these times in my life, you know, she'd say, 'Wait 'til you get kids. Wait until you become a mother.' You know. Somehow I got the feeling it's tied in with her somewhere.

So, very early in her treatment, we find Anna proposing that the symptom which brought her for clinical help is, in some as yet unspecified way, connected to her childhood experience of being taken to school for the first time by her father and separated from her mother. Separation from her mother is introduced here as a central component of that experience.

Session 41

Anna returns to this event again in the 41st session. Here, for the first time, she tells a fully narrated account of her experience. She is telling the analyst about a period in her childhood when she and her parents lived with her grandparents. She describes her grandparents' home as a lively place, full of people, activity, and attention. The analyst says:

> So there were an awful lot of grownups around and you were a pretty little girl. . . . and they paid a lot of attention to you.

Anna responds "Yes, that was" and goes on to tell her story.

> And then all of a sudden, you know, you move out of there and–they get their own house and another baby comes along and then another baby comes along a year after that and you're shoved off to school and your mother doesn't even take you, your father takes you–the one who yelled at you, you know, when the first baby came, you know. I think all of these are elements you know–that kinda made my attitude I guess.

Here the event is set in the context of more profound separations and losses, moving out of her grandparent's home, the birth of siblings. Anna's phrase "shoved off to school" conveys for the first time her affective experience of being forcibly separated.

In her description of her father as "the one who yelled" Anna introduces the problematic nature of her relationship with her father. Her experience of this event involves not just separation from mother ("mother didn't take me"), but being taken by a father who yells.

In this narrative Anna employs the second person as a linguistic device. Her use of the second person "you" to refer to herself, and her shift to the first person "I think" to introduce the final evaluative clause, provide emphasis and highlight the content of the story. Anna returns, in this narrated account, to the phrase "your mother doesn't take you to school, your father takes you." These clauses, like the body of the narrative, are in the second person; their message is strengthened by their linguistic structure.

Session 44

In session 44 Anna tells her analyst that she has asked her mother for an account of the event. She says:

> I talked with my mother. . . . I mentioned that I can't remember her being at a lot of things or a lot of–like–like take–I says, 'You didn't take me the first day of school, did you?' She said, 'No,' she didn't, that 'daddy did,' that she wasn't feeling good. She was sick.

In this retelling Anna uses quoted speech, her own and her mother's, for emphasis to highlight her account. The phrases "you didn't take me" and "daddy did" reappear in this retelling as quoted speech.

Anna goes on to describe several other experiences which involved her father doing things for or with her in her mother's absence, and concludes:

> and, oh, just a lot of things that, uh, [sighs] kinda the mother wasn't around, my father was around and my father–in the Navy, he was a chief petty officer and my mother says that he's a lousy teacher. He yells and screams and doesn't know how to be calm.

In this session the dual themes "my mother didn't take me, my father took me" are explored. Anna seeks to account for her mother's absence–her general feeling that her "mother wasn't around"–by asking her mother for an explanation, and simultaneously elaborates her experience of her father's presence–"he was around," but his presence was problematic. Anna's statement that "he yells and screams and doesn't know how to be calm" provides an elaboration of her description of him in the previous retelling (session 41) as "the one who yelled."

Session 52

Anna adds detail and richness to this picture of her father when, in session 52, she returns again to consideration of the event.

For the first time, in this session, she links this past experience with a specific incident of fearfulness and phobic symptoms in the present. She says, speaking about her recent difficulty taking her son to school when accompanied by her husband:

> this going out business, I thought maybe [sighs] when I get afraid– maybe I'm reliving something like when I had to take (son) to school

and I got so worked up [blows nose] I thought maybe it's the time when I was first going to school and my father was taking me maybe I used (husband) as my father–he's so cold, you know. He's not emotionally understanding.

The analyst asks "and how did you connect that with your father?" and she responds with her thematic phrase "Well, my father took me the first time to school, my mother didn't." When the analyst asks "Is he cold then?" she enlarges her description of her father and her experience with him:

Well I don't remember any–yeah–You gotta go. Get in line. Just go. You know, no–no explanation–just . . (the analyst responds) No support and encouragement.

Right. No like–like you'll get out at such and such a time and you'll come home and you're going to have a good time and you're going to learn things and I mean, . . . (the analyst responds) Sink or swim.

Right. Cut and dried. C-P-O-or C-P–what it would be–Chief Petty Officer–CPO–you know.

She focuses, in this retelling, on what was missing in her experience, on her father's inability to provide the explanation and support she needed on her first day of school, and on his characteristic abruptness ("cut and dried") which she again associates (as in session 44) with his position as a naval CPO.

Session 58

In session 58 Anna provides a second fully narrated account of her experience. She tells this narrative in the context of linking her phobic symptoms in the present with her childhood experience. This is the second time in these retellings she has made such a link (see session 44). In this session, Anna describes her attempts to avoid her usual fearfulness and physical symptoms while visiting friends with her husband the previous Saturday night. Trying to understand her present fearfulness, she searches for some past event which would clarify her experience. She says:

I keep trying to remember maybe something with–with, uh, my father and I going somewhere or something and, uh, I don't know. Do children bury feelings that they just refuse to remember or they

> just don't think they remember them or [sighs] 'cause I can't remember–I really can't. I just–total nothing when it comes to that–that, uh [sighs] trying to remember my father and myself.

The recollection which follows is Anna's second fully narrated account of this experience.

> All I remember is just–I guess, the first day of school and I kinda remember him walking and I can hear his voice but I don't remember him as much [sighs] but I didn't like it. I didn't like being separated. I–I don't think the first week or so was that bad to go to school but, I think after that, I [sighs] started gettin' all that throwing up or–maybe that's a symptom I used to get out of going to school– someplace I didn't want to go. I'd rather stay at home. Yeah. I would have rather stayed at home.

This narrative, like the one in session 41, places the event in a richer context. While the earlier narrative told us what preceded this crucial first day of school (the move from grandparent's home, the birth of siblings) this one tells us what followed,–"I started all that throwing up"–the emergence of her symptom. Here the vomiting is linked explicitly with Anna's wish to avoid separation, her unwillingness to leave home.

In this narrative Anna sensitively explores her affective response to the event. While the second person account in the earlier narrative served to emphasize content, it also distanced it from the narrator. Here, Anna's use of the first person, the tentativeness of her memory ("I kinda remember" and her use of the present tense ("I can hear his voice") intensify the immediacy of the narrative. Her first person statements about her feelings are almost childlike in their simplicity "I didn't like it. I didn't like being separated." Her final statement, "I'd rather stay at home. Yeah. I would have rather stayed at home," in its shift from present to past tense, conveys both the child's voice and the adult woman's reflection on it.

Session 117

Anna's third narrative retelling of this event occurs in session 117. It is the longest and most complex telling in the treatment. This narrative accomplishes two things: first, it provides a retelling of the event itself which integrates all the aspects which had been explored and developed in the previous tellings, and second, it coherently and compellingly forges a link between the narrated event and the symptom which brought Anna to treatment.

Anna introduces the narrative by mentioning an article on phobias she'd read recently. She says:

> I read some article. I'll never be able to quote it right. Where that having a phobia, you resort back to some gimmick you used when you were little to get attention or something.

The analyst asks what the article meant to her. Anna's reply takes the form of a narrative.

> Well I thought—all right, that time I had to go to first grade and everything and my father took me 'cause I guess my mother had the baby to take care of, uh, maybe I was really naturally scared to be separated and there was no reassurance from anybody—except go and—and it was kinda like a very lost feeling, like, uh, nobody really cares, you know, so if you get sick—I don't know—it just seemed to happen that way where you end up throwing up, you know, you just get so nervous and scared that you end up throwing up. And, uh, then they care 'bout you, you know, you're sick. Oh, didn't I say that my mother was a Florence Nightingale when we were sick—definitely true. When we're sick she's right there at our bedside. Uh—you know, maybe I found out—I don't remember what happened those days. I just—I remember some incidents and some incidents I don't where— where I did get scared and I did throw up and I never made it to school, I ended up staying home—I got to stay home. I guess—I guess I wasn't separated from parents or some—it's very vague.

Structurally Anna begins this narrative with a first person account of her experience. The tone of this account is tentative and speculative ("I thought," "I guess," "maybe") as befits a heuristic narrative (Robinson, 1981). Anna's goal, in retelling this narrative, is to fully understand her childhood experience and to understand how that experience is related to her symptoms as an adult. She is questioning and unsure. Her understanding develops and/or emerges in the course of this narration.

The thematic phrases "My father took me," "my mother didn't" reappear here in elaborated form, "My father took me, 'cause I guess my mother had the baby to take care of." This understanding of her mother's absence emerges from and represents an integration of questions raised and issues addressed in previous retellings. In session 41, for example, her feelings of loss around separation beginning school are linked with the birth of siblings. In the retelling in session 44 Anna confronts her mother about her absence. The statement "I guess my mother had the baby to take care of" replaces the statement "my mother didn't take me" with an explanatory account which represents a new synthesis of Anna's understanding and, perhaps, a resolution of sorts of her questions about this critical absence. In this narrative Anna notes the simultaneity of her two separations from mother–the one, an emotional separation caused by her displacement by a new sibling, and the other, a more concrete, physical separation, resulting from her entering school. The continuity in time of these two separations suggest that Anna's memory of her first day of school might serve, at least in part, as a "screen" or metaphor for the more profound emotional separation resulting from the birth of her sister. The relationship between these two events (mother's absence on the first day is due to the presence of a new baby) is clearly articulated for the first time in this narrative.

The parallel theme around father's presence (my father took me) is also elaborated in this retelling. This theme had been explored and developed previously (in sessions 41, 44, 52, and 58.) Anna's emphasis in these earlier retellings had been on her father's inability to provide her with support and encouragement, on his "cut and dried" response to her emotional needs. Her statement "there was no reassurance from anybody–except go" echoes her description in session 52. However in this retelling her accompanying feelings of fear and loss are richly described for the first time. The depth and affective intensity of Anna's description in this narrative ("it was kind a like a very lost feeling, like uh nobody really cares") contrasts with the simplicity, and relative superficiality, of her earlier (session 58) description ("I didn't like it. I didn't like being separated"). In this later account Anna is more attuned to the richness and complexity of her own response.

In the next passage of the narrative Anna shifts to the third person to describe the early, natural link between her anxiety and her symptom ("you just get so nervous and scared that you end up throwing up") and the function it served for her as a child ("then they care about you"). This is a succinct, coherent statement describing the origin of her symptom in her early fearfulness about loss and separation and its function in restoring her to her mother's care. It represents an elaboration of her beginning speculations about the function of her symptom in session 58 ("maybe that's a symptom I used to get out of going to school–someplace I didn't want to go"). The emphasis here, however, is on securing care and avoiding separation, rather than on avoiding school.

Anna's concluding statement in the narrative, an evaluative aside in which she returns to the first person ("Oh, didn't I say that my mother was a Florence Nightingale when we were sick. . . . ") explains the appropriateness of her symptom choice. Her mother was a "Florence Nightingale"; illness transformed her absence (my mother didn't take me) to presence ("she's right there by our bedside").

In the conclusion of the narrative Anna returns to her exploratory, speculative first person account ("I don't remember," "I guess–I guess," "it's very vague"). In this continuation she links the initial event with a series of vaguely remembered subsequent events in which getting sick permitted her to miss school and avoid separation. These events are described as an example of the "gimmick she used" as a child to "get attention" and avoid separation. Anna makes clear, in this narrative account, that she understands that as a child she used vomiting to maintain connection and avoid separation. In her preamble to this narrative she links this motive with her present phobic symptoms; they are a "gimmick she resorts back to."

When we compare this fully developed narrative account of Anna's experience with her first mention of the event in session 6, the dynamic nature of the narrative process in this clinical treatment becomes obvious. Each retelling has introduced new elements and/or elaborated existing dimensions of the story. All of these aspects are integrated in Anna's narrative account in session 117. But this narrative goes beyond integration to achieve a deeper more complex understanding of the meaning of Anna's childhood experience of being taken to school by her father on the first day and its relevance to the phobic symptoms which brought her to treatment.

This paper has thus far described Anna's exploration of this one childhood experience as it relates to themes of separation and connection, themes which could be described as "preoedipal." The careful reader will have noted that our sequential account has omitted reference to Anna's retelling in session 81. This omission was made in the interest of clarity and coherence, but as clinicians we are aware that clarity and coherence are more often the result of editing and re-construction–as they are here– than reflective of the realities of clinical discourse. In session 81 Anna and the analyst begin to explore an additional set of meanings embedded in her experience of being taken to school for the first time by her father. In this session, and sessions 152 and 159, Anna reflects on the sexual aspects of her childhood relationship with her father, on echoes of "oedipal" themes which may be relevant to understanding her story.

Sexual Themes: Sessions 81, 152, 159

In session 81 Anna suggests that her phobic symptoms may perform an important function in the present. The sexual content of the transference had been a recent topic in the treatment. Anna describes an incident in which she had pursued a sexual fantasy about the analyst and had a strong phobic reaction; she had gotten physically ill and the fantasy had ended abruptly. She suggests "maybe the phobia is a kind of shaking me up, you know, to keep my sex in control, possibly." The analyst responds enthusiastically to this suggestion. Anna struggles to link this new understanding with her experience of phobic symptoms when taking her son to school. She says:

> That's what really confuses me, in a way–'cause what's so–what's such a sex element about taking your son to this, uh–where we go–register him for that performing arts at that high school, you know, what–you know, here's (husband) and (son) and I . . . I mean, what's–what's, you know, the sex element there?

The analyst proposes a resolution:

> Well you just gave me–gave me an idea–don't know if it's right but I'll try. The way you said what's sexual about taking your son–and it occurred to me that maybe a mother taking a son–in a very special way–in the way you wanted your father to take you–may have awakened thoughts somehow in you of a father taking a daughter–you understand what I mean.

Anna makes the link to the specific event we have been tracking, her experience of being taken to school on the first day by her father. She responds:

> I get the feeling that uh, put it as me being a little girl and my father being the parent–the father and say the idea of him taking me to first grade the first time, there was the wish or the want to be protected by him–not to be separated by him because actually I know him more than where I was going and yet in there was–I don't know how you put it but how you attach–there's some sex element in there somewhere somehow.

Here she acknowledges the importance of attachment and separation in her experience of this event, but also acknowledges that it may have had a sexual component. Again, the analyst proposes an interpretation:

> You know, that's an interesting thought you just voiced because you have emphasized in the past–my father took me and that was wrong,

it should have been my mother right? . . . Maybe the reason that you return to that memory from time to time is for the reason that you are just now saying–that in some way the idea of his taking you was connected up unconsciously in your mind with something inappropriate between a father and a daughter.

Here the leitmotif "My father took me," "My mother didn't take me" acquires an additional, sexualized meaning.

Anna's response to the analyst's interpretation, the flood of questions and associations which follow, her struggle and confusion, suggest that his idea resonates for her. She says:

I mean, is that natural. I mean is that normal for people–I mean, or . . . suppose there were tendencies or wishes of–I don't know what–what could you possibly have at five years old, I mean, what–I mean, you really don't know, you're not aware of, uh, actual sex elements of, you know, making love–what the heck could–could–I mean, is your body tuned to have those little, uh, feelings–what am I talking about? I mean, I've read babies masturbate and so forth and all this. This is what (sighs) you know, just–could there be the awareness that–that– that sense (sighs) . . .

The structure of this response, its disjointed quality, the repeated starts and stops, the questioning, repetition of phrases ("you know," "I don't know," "I mean") and self observation ("What am I talking about?"), all are markers of the emotional intensity of the content. Anna's question "what could you possibly have at five years old," her recognition of infantile sexuality ("babies masturbate"), her worry about whether this is "normal," and the acknowledgement of, and questions about, her guilt, speak convincingly of a childhood (oedipal) sexual dilemma.

Session 152

In session 152 Anna returns to her earlier theme of her need for support and nurturance, her wish that her mother would provide them, and her anger at her mother's failure. These needs have, predictably, emerged in the transference relationship with the analyst. Anna says to him:

You could be taking her place in a way, (sighs) what about this–this– I've given thought to that–that element that my father's like two parents rolled up into one (sighs) (pause). You know, recalling to mind, many times where I wish he wasn't doing or taking me wherever I had to go (sighs) you know. That I guess there was a need to be understood or–or given security to and it wasn't there–it was just cut and dry–too cold (sighs). I don't know. That's probably why I resent my mother so much.

She describes again her feelings about being taken by her father ("I wish he wasn't doing or taking me") and his inability to provide the warmth and support she craved as a child. The phrases she uses, "cold," "cut and dry," echo descriptions from earlier sessions.

Anna's focus here is on the theme of dependence and separation, but the analyst shifts this focus when he asks, "Did you ever have the feeling your father forced himself on you sort of?" Anna's immediate response to this query ignores the potential sexual implications of the phrase "forced himself on you." She denies that this was the case and cites her discussion with her mother.

No. I have asked my mother about certain things like, uh, how come she didn't take me the first day of school and she said, "Well, I was sick." She didn't feel good . . . my dad took me places like that . . . you know, she's always had some element of an excuse . . . I don't know, I–I think both my parents that really, uh, my mom didn't want to do a lot of things. She shifted the burden for a lot of things . . .

She concludes "[sigh] I know it's all very mixed up." In her response Anna focuses on her mother's inability and/or unwillingness to meet her needs, on the absence of nurture rather than the presence of a sexual component as central to the meaning of this experience. But, despite her denial, the associations which follow lend credibility to a possible sexual meaning.

In comments immediately following her denial, Anna describes her response to an article in a woman's magazine she'd read the previous week:

the article is titled, "Are you seducing your child or children?" And I read that Friday evening and after I read the article, I was really somewhat hostile to my father–I was thinking all these–I was saying to myself–I'll be damned, I think this is what he was doing. I think he was really doing this to me. Uh, I was mad after that point, I was . . .

The analyst asks "Now just what do you mean by saying he was seducing you?" Anna answers:

Well, just–just–the hitting me and the way he was talking and–the
way he handled himself when I think about it. (sighs) . . . not–not
physically–not with intercourse but–but mentally like. That–I think,
more or less, that's the way the article was written, mentally seducing.

Though Anna does not consciously feel that her father "forced himself" on her in taking her to school, she does feel that he was seductive in
his relationship with her.

Session 159

In session 159 Anna struggles to understand the sexual aspects of her
relationship with her father. She clearly articulates her confusion:

How does a daughter get that hung up on a father–I mean, even
sexually, I mean, how the heck does that ever come about I mean,
uh–I mean, especially when there were no such physical actions–no
such, uh–you know, factual–you know, really things going on. I
mean, just because he hits you–just because he yells at you–you
twist that around and turn it into what you want. It just doesn't seem
to be possible. I mean, it seems possible but it doesn't make sense.

The analyst provides an interpretation in the form of a summary narrative. This narrative has clearly emerged in the course of their work together. He says:

I think you're forgetting how it began. I think what you're forgetting
is that it began when you were a very little girl and when your
relationship with your father was extremely pleasurable. And then
came the terrible disappointment when you felt he turned away from
you. As you, yourself, have pointed out–the only major kind of
relationship you had with him after that was one in which you felt
hurt and hit and scolded and all the rest of it . . . So what happened
was, I think, that later relationship became the only form in which
you felt you could recapture the early one–that's why it took on that
meaning.

In the extended discussion which follows, Anna provides her own
account of this shift from closeness with her father to hitting and scolding.

It's very human to think–I think–I hope I'm thinking this right–uh,
all the words, all the touching, all the feelings–like in the first five

> years, are human. I mean, are very human, uh, to be accepted. And the second part–the other after that, (sighs) I mean, it's completely cut off and then things are introduced such as yelling and spanking, scolding and scorning and belittling and so forth and so forth . . . . I just–I can't understand it. I just–you know, I try to say logically– responsibility, children (sighs) but I mean, it–it sure seems like a total cut off. I mean, really just (clicking sound with tongue) I mean– I'm trying to say–well he took me to school and he took me to the dentist and he–what–that's about it–that's all I can think of . . .

Here the element of separation and loss, of being "cut off" is introduced in an oedipal context; the loss here is of closeness with father.

(If we apply a stereotypical drive theory model, Anna's use of the phrase "completely cut off" might suggest an interpretation around concern about castration. However, in the context of this treatment, being "cut off" from love and support seem primary. Pushing the data to conform with a theoretical model would, in my opinion, distort it–and would also distort and oversimplify the theory. The fact that the analyst doesn't choose to pursue this line supports this view.)

As Anna reflects on the change in her relationship with her father, on feeling "cut off" from him, she returns to her experience of being taken to school by him for the first time. Anna's phrase "not to let it seem that way" speaks to her wish to deny the changed nature of their relationship. Her statement "Well he took me to school" lays claim to a continuation of their early bond, and attempts to deny that she was "cut off" from him. But, as Anna acknowledges, these attempts at denial have been unsuccessful. The analyst refers to Anna's recurring statement, her leitmotif, "My father took me. My mother didn't" and proposes an explanation for the shift in her father's treatment of her. He says:

> I think there's something you may be omitting. That is–we talked about this too but I think it's pertinent again. You have described your father as doing a lot of things for you that ordinarily, a mother does . . . My idea is that maybe your father was more interested in you than you realized but that your father felt guilty about it and that also had something to do with the way he treated you so that he disguised his real feelings by his distorted way of scolding and hitting and all the rest of it and one of the reasons that seems to be, to me, important is because I think that you show the same thing here with me.

The analyst suggests that her father's withdrawal from her, his "scolding and hitting," were a reaction against his strong–perhaps sexual–interest in her, an interest that made him feel guilty.

An extended discussion of Anna's sexual feelings, in the transference and with her own children, and the importance of accepting and managing sexual feelings without distorting them and withdrawing–as her father did–follows. Though in this discussion explicit links are not made to Anna's present use of phobic symptoms to manage and control her sexual feelings, these links seem relevant. Until Anna can consciously acknowledge and control her sexual feelings (for example, for her son and the analyst) she may need to resort to phobic symptoms to provide this function, as she describes doing in session 81.

The sexualized "oedipal" themes in the treatment, as they relate to Anna's experience on the first day of school, are developed and elaborated in sessions 81, 152, and 159, but then fall from view. This content is not referred to in subsequent retellings; there is no further mention of this content in relation to Anna's story. We can only speculate about its absence. Perhaps, in these three sessions the "oedipal" theme was adequately developed in relation to this material and neither Anna nor the analyst felt the need to reintroduce it in this context. This theme may, then, be dealt with in relation to other content; its invisibility may be due only to our sampling methods.

It may be important to note that the analyst was unusually active in introducing and elaborating this thematic material. When, in session 81, he responds enthusiastically to Anna's interpretation of her phobia as functioning "to keep my sex in control" she comments "Boy, you jumped on that one." Perhaps he has consciously decided not to be so active in relation to raising this thematic content in later sessions. Or perhaps, as a result of their mutual exploration of Anna's sexual feelings in the transference, both the analyst and Anna have backed away from this potentially difficult content. Without a more comprehensive examination of the data than is possible within the framework of this research, it is impossible to reach any conclusions. What we do know, however, is that in the four final retellings of Anna's experience on the first day of school, the focus returns once again to issues of separation and loss.

The sessions that have been outlined thus far occurred during a fourteen month period. In the remaining twenty months of the treatment, Anna and the analyst return to this event only four additional times, in sessions 173, 252, 269, and 305. In session 173 Anna narrates the event for the last time. She begins by describing her childhood pattern of vomiting before or during elementary school. She then tells her now familiar story.

> I don't remember vomiting for that first day of school my dad took
> me. I remember being miserable and upset and didn't want to go and
> he didn't help by saying it would be all right there. He just—go—like
> getting rid of you and not telling you that that's a good place to be.
> You know they leave out half of it, it seems like, you know, but I
> think that's part of a parent's responsibility to let a child know that
> they are going to a good place and that the parent isn't getting rid of
> them or getting them out of their hair.

The factual, referential, and evaluative components of this narrative account are familiar. Anna's emphasis is on her father's failure to provide
what she needed. This is content which has been explored previously;
there is nothing new here.

Similarly, Anna's commentary on her story in session 252 represents a
restatement of earlier material. Her focus here is on her mother's unwillingness to be involved with her and meet her needs. But nothing new is
added to her previous formulation. What is unique about this retelling is
that it is the analyst who initially refers to the event. In the context of
discussing Anna's mother's failure to care for her adequately, the analyst is
"reminded of another . . . a number of things that you really have said—
about your father doing things that you think your mother should have
done." Anna refers to one such event and the analyst asks "And did he not
take you to school?" In this session, for the first time, it is the analyst who
initially refers to this seminal event; it has become an element of their
shared narrative.

In session 269 Anna focuses on her confusion as a child and links this
confusion with her fearfulness about going out. She says "a lot of that
confusion led to being scared to death of things." She then refers briefly to
going to first grade as an example, a time when her confusion about what
was happening, and her father's inability to explain and provide support, led
her to be fearful. Finally, in session 305, three months before the end of the
treatment, Anna returns to this event for the final time. She is reminded of it
in the course of describing a frightening childhood fall. The analyst says:

> I think the fall also took place in a situation in which you felt locked
> out by your parent—partly because of the arrival of a new baby and
> partly because of the way they behaved when you did . . .

He links her experience of falling with being "locked out by" her parents
and with the birth of a sibling, experiences of separation which had previously been associated with Anna's experience on her first day of school.
In response to the analyst's comments Anna says:

Then too, it reminded me of uh my mother not going with me to school, you know. Sending me alone all the time–or with my dad. I didn't like that.

Anna's final account of this event mirrors her initial account in its simplicity. Here, however, the analyst provides the missing evaluative commentary. He links this particular event with Anna's pervasive experience of separation and loss, and links it with her present fearfulness when she's "afraid of going someplace." He says:

It was a separation from your mother and the feeling that your mother was not taking adequate care of you and that feeling has apparently persisted so that when you become afraid to go someplace, you're like a child who's being asked to do something that's beyond her capacity and whose parents won't help.

This statement by the analyst briefly summarizes the work they have done together around this one story. The understanding which has emerged from Anna's multiple retellings, which the analyst privileges in his final summary, is that this was, in its essence, an experience of separation and loss, an experience of not being cared for, and that this early experience reverberates for Anna in her present fearfulness about going out, and is expressed in her phobic symptoms.

Here, as the treatment draws to a close, the analyst presents a streamlined, thematic summary of their work together around this narrative. The more elaborate formulations and linkages made in earlier sessions (see especially session 117) are only referenced here, but this succinct statement of theme, and Anna's understanding of it–her affective/experiential as well as cognitive grasp of this content–are possible only as a result of their shared work around this entire series of retellings.

CONCLUSION

This microanalysis of the telling and retelling of one client story over a 2 1/2 year analysis can only suggest the complexity and dynamic nature of the narrative process in this clinical treatment. In order to fully appreciate the richness of this process, it would be necessary to place the narrative process described here for this one story in the context of the interacting web of the telling and retelling of many stories. The work around Anna's retelling of her first-day-of-school narrative has functioned in conjunction with work around the retelling of other related events with similar thematic content which have surfaced repeatedly in connection with this story. (It would be possible to list three of four events which were consistently referenced in relation to Anna's retelling of her-first-day-of-school narrative.) To understand the true complexity of the narrative process in this treatment, it would be necessary to trace each of these interwoven stories and to describe how change in the understanding and formulation of one event reverberated through Anna's understanding of the other narratives.

To fully grasp the complexity of narrative process in this case, it would also be necessary to place work with this one narrative in the context of the transference within which it unfolded. Though in this paper the focus has been on narrative process, it is important to note that the elaboration of Anna's narrative and the exploration of the transference relationship occur together in a reflexive process. The emergence of issues in the transference parallels and enriches Anna's developing understanding of her narrative, as the exploration of narrative meanings clarifies the transference relationship. In sessions 81 and 159, for example, Anna's understanding of the oedipal content of the narrative emerges in the context of her exploration of sexualized aspects of the transference relationship. In session 152 it is the exploration of maternal elements of her transferential relationship with the analyst which lead back to consideration of the narrative. (While Anna's sexualized paternal [oedipal] transference to the analyst and her maternal nurturant [preoedipal] transference are explored and related to the meaning of her story, there is no discussion, within these sessions, of a possible preoedipal paternal transference. Neither Anna nor the analyst explore Anna's possible experience of him as, like her father and her husband, "cold," unsupportive, "cut and dry.")

Structure of Narrative Process

If, having acknowledged the importance of these contextual issues, we persist in our "single case" focus, we can identify three moments or phases in the structure of the narrative process: first, the initial telling in which the facts of the story were presented with little elaboration (session 6), second, a period of on-going discussion in which affect was explored, the surrounding context was elaborated, and the meaning of the event emerged from the dialogue between Anna and the analyst (sessions 17, 41, 44, 52, 58). This phase of the process culminated in the telling of a vastly enriched and expanded version of the narrative which integrated all the aspects which had been previously explored (session 117). Retelling and discussion of the narrative was most frequent during this second phase. During the third phase of the narrative process, the richly elaborated narrative was distilled to its essential components. The process of unpacking and elaborating the context and meaning of the story ended. Anna's retellings in this phase lack the searching, heuristic quality of retellings during the second phase. A more schematic, simplified version of the story emerged, reflecting a shared understanding of the meaning this event had for Anna.

During this third phase, both Anna and the analyst refer back to the event in abbreviated form to illustrate or support points being made in the on-going treatment. It is as if the work of understanding this event had been accomplished, and could be used as a resource in the continuing process of treatment. Anna's final account of this event, in session 305, is as simple as her initial retelling. However, it is followed by an evaluative summary provided by the analyst which effectively condenses the central meaning of the story which had emerged from their joint effort to understand. The fact that this story was not mentioned again suggests that perhaps there was nothing left to say about it; it had been understood.

Anna's narrative, as described here, moves from simplicity, through complexity, and back to simplicity. However, the simplicity which is regained is at a higher level of understanding; it represents a distillation of the richly elaborated narrative content. The simplified story functions as a symbol for, or contains, the elaborated content. It provides a mechanism for referencing that content in abbreviated form.

Content of Narrative Process

Our description has documented the emergence and elaboration of two central themes in the content of this narrative. Anna's narrative, like her symptoms, appears to be multiply determined. Her experience of being taken to school on the first day by her father is salient because it embodies both oedipal (my father took me) and preoedipal (my mother didn't take me) dilemmas. These issues co-exist and co-determine her strong response to and memory of this event. In the treatment, Anna uses her memory of this one event to explore her childhood experience around dependency, separation and loss, and sexualized aspects of her relationship with her father. This one event clearly has meaning for Anna at different developmental levels.

What is perplexing is the rapidity with which one of these central themes—the one involving sexualized content—disappears from the narrative process. While meanings involving issues of attachment and separation are explored in seven sessions and referenced in three additional ones over a thirty month period, the oedipal theme is explored in only three sessions, over seven months, and then disappears from the dialogue. Though we have speculated about the cause of this disappearance, its meaning remains unresolved.

BIBLIOGRAPHY

Agger, J. & Jensen, S. (1990). Testimony as ritual and evidence in psychotherapy for political refugees. *Journal of Traumatic Stress*, *5*, 115-136.

Boudwyns, P.A., Meyer, L., Woods, M.G., Harrison, W. R. & McCranie, E. (1990). PTSD among Vietnamese veterans: An early look at treatment outcome using direct therapeutic exposure. *Journal of Traumatic Stress*, *3*, 359-368.

Cienfuegos, A. & Monelli, C. (1983). The testimony of political repression as a therapeutic instrument. *American Journal of Orthopsychiatry*, *53*, 43-51.

Herman, J. (1992). *Trauma & Recovery*. New York: Basic Books.

Herman, J. & Schatzow, E. (1987). Recovering and verification of memories of childhood sexual trauma. *Psychoanalytic Psychology*, *4*, 1-14.

Labov, W. & Waletsky, J. (1967). Narrative analysis: oral versions of personal experience. In J. Helm (Ed.), *Essays in the Verbal & Visual Arts*. Seattle: American Ethnological Society.

Miller, P. (1993). Troubles in the garden and how they get resolved: a young child's transformation of his favorite story. In Charles A. Nelson (Ed.), *Memory & Affect in Development: Minnesota Symposium on Child Psychology*. Vol. 26, Hillsdale, NJ: Erlbaum.

Nye, C. (1994). Narrative interaction & the development of client autonomy in clinical practice. *Clinical Social Work Journal*, Vol. 22, No. 1, Spring 1994.

Nye, C. (1993). Screen memories. *Readings: A Journal of Reviews & Commentary in Mental Health*, June 1993, *8*(2), 12-17.

Robinson, J. A. (1981). Personal narratives reconsidered. *Journal of American Folklore*, *94*(371), 58-85.

Terr, L. (1981). 'Forbidden games' post traumatic child's play. *Journal of the American Academy of Child Psychology*. *20*, 741-760.

Terr, L. (1988). What happens to early memories of trauma: a study of 20 children under age 5 at the time of documented traumatic events. *Journal of the American Academy of Child & Adolescent Psychiatry*, *27*, 96-104.

Chapter 7

Using Narrative Theory and Self Psychology Within a Multigenerational Family Systems Perspective

Thomas M. Young

SUMMARY. This paper illustrates how a process of psychoanalytic psychotherapy can be enhanced and extended by combining ideas from narrative theory and self psychology within a multigenerational family systems perspective. The illustration is based on a summary and discussion of a satisfactorily completed thirty-session psychotherapy for an adult man who sought therapy for relief from his depression. *[Article copies available from The Haworth Document Delivery Service: 1-800-342-9678. E-mail address: getinfo@haworth.com].*

INTRODUCTION

As the title suggests, this paper attempts to connect certain ideas from narrative theory with others from self psychology and organize them within a multigenerational family systems perspective. In doing so, I hope to illustrate how the process of psychoanalytic psychotherapy can be enhanced by extending its reach both cognitively and intergenerationally.

Address correspondence to Thomas M. Young, PhD, Widener University, Center for Social Work Education, Chester, PA 19013.

[Haworth co-indexing entry note]: "Using Narrative Theory and Self Psychology Within a Multigenerational Family Systems Perspective." Young, Thomas M. Co-published simultaneously in *Journal of Analytic Social Work* (The Haworth Press, Inc.) Vol. 3, No. 2/3, 1996, pp. 137-155; and: *Narration and Therapeutic Action: The Construction of Meaning in Psychoanalytic Social Work* (ed: Jerrold R. Brandell) The Haworth Press, Inc., 1996, pp. 137-155. Single or multiple copies of this article are available from The Haworth Document Delivery Service [1-800-342-9678, 9:00 a.m. - 5:00 p.m. (EST) E-mail address: get info@haworth.com].

137

For the purpose of this paper, I understand the phrase "process of psychoanalytic psychotherapy" in a context provided by self psychology (Kohut, 1971, 1977, 1984). It refers to both the interpersonal and intrapsychic aspects of a therapeutic conversation: a dialogue organized around a mutually arrived at understanding of the client in psychological depth. This dialogue is facilitated by the therapist through what the Ornstein's have described as the empathic mode of listening and the interpretive mode of speaking (Ornstein, A. & Ornstein, P., 1990). This process, when it works, typically leaves the client feeling more integrated cognitively, emotionally, and behaviorally; more focused, energized, productive, and alive; more able to relate to others in a genuine and satisfying way. Usually, as the client's self becomes more robust, the presenting symptoms, complaints, or problems recede or become resolved.

To extend this process cognitively via narrative theory means explicitly acknowledging that in a fundamental way all of the conversations we call therapy are constructions–stories that are inherently partial or incomplete. It also implies an understanding that all of these audible, or public, conversations and the stories they narrate are related to concurrent private (internal, unspoken) conversations that therapists and clients each have with themselves. In narrative therapy terms, the client's private story about himself is assumed to have a strong influence on his feelings and actions. Psychotherapy, then, is a process of "re-storying" or "re-authoring" the private story carried by the client so that the client is less oppressed and more empowered by it in his living (White & Epston, 1990, 1992; White, 1995). Of course, the same is true for the therapist but that is another paper (Horner, 1995).

To extend this process intergenerationally means to acknowledge explicitly that both the client's story and ways of living shaped by that story are influenced by the multigenerational family system. The content, structure, and meanings of all our stories are imbedded in the culture and history of our families and can only be discerned and examined in that multigenerational context. In the multigenerational family systems theory developed by Bowen (1976), our difficulties with ourselves and others are viewed as rooted in how losses within the multigenerational family system have influenced our process of intrapsychic and interpersonal differentiation.

A multigenerationally oriented therapy is a process of repositioning one's self (cognitively, emotionally, and behaviorally) vis-à-vis others by balancing the sadness and anxiety related to those losses with the wisdom and support derived from re-established or re-constituted relationships with family members both living and deceased (Freeman, 1992a: 209ff; 1992b: 205ff).

To facilitate the illustration and discussion of using these theories in practice, I begin by providing some background on the client and the initial phase of the therapy in which my participation as therapist was guided by ideas taken from both narrative theory and self psychology and organized within a multigenerational systems perspective. Following that, I set forth what I understand to be the central tenets of narrative theory, self psychology, and the multigenerational family systems perspective, as articulated by Bowen and Freeman. Then the summary and discussion of the therapeutic process resumes, covering the conclusion of the initial phase as well as the middle and ending phases.

OVERVIEW OF CASE

The therapeutic process involved a 30-session, twice monthly psychotherapy for Mr. F., who sought out individual therapy for himself in the hope of gaining some relief from his depression and acquiring a greater sense of "personal agency and integration," as he put it. He was in his mid-forties and had both an academic and an administrative appointment at a university. He was very knowledgeable about postmodernist thinking (Gergen, 1991; Bruner, 1986, 1990; Pardeck, Murphy, & Choi, 1994).

From his own work in his academic specialization, he was already familiar with the constructivist and deconstructivist perspectives and the central role of storying within them. He was comfortable with the notion of alternative stories or interpretations depending on the perspective of the narrator, the role of discourse or conversation in the creation of meaning, and the central contribution of context to understanding anything. All of these are basic concepts underlying narrative theory.

His older brother, Jerry, had died shortly after birth. For his parents, this loss of their firstborn child was literally unspeakable. In fact, it was not spoken of in Mr. F.'s presence until at age 12 he accidently discovered Jerry's baby book. For Mr. F.'s father it echoed his own older brother's death from drowning during their adolescence while they were swimming together. The loss of his own firstborn son was made more poignant by the fact that he and his wife had named their newborn baby after the deceased uncle. Thus, the presence of loss in the multigenerational family system was evident from the beginning.

In the initial session he expressed a desire for a greater sense of personal agency and integration, suggesting an "enfeebled self" or "depletion state" from a self-psychological perspective (Kohut & Wolf, 1978; Palombo, 1985). In addition, it was possible to notice indications of a continuing yearning for the self-selfobject experiences of appreciation (mirroring), inspiration (idealizing), and collegiality (twinship).

Mr. F. was seeking psychotherapy for relief from his depression, believing now that he had been depressed all of his life. He suspected he ought to consider a trial on antidepressant medication. But he had two prior episodes of psychotherapy that he had found helpful and he knew he had "more work to do" especially with respect to his father, now deceased. What troubled him was that he felt that he did not really know his father, what kind of man he was. Mostly he recalled him as "alcoholic and depressed; loving but distant." I sensed the need for an idealizing experience in this.

He knew that I too was an academic and we slipped easily into a collegial mode of talking about how his depression had interfered with his writing for publication since completing his doctoral dissertation nearly ten years earlier. Then, when relating the information about the deaths of his own and his father's brother, he remarked that he missed having a brother. From this I understood a possible need for a twinship/alter-ego experience.

And from his very first statement that he was seeking "a greater sense of personal agency and integration," I sensed the need for some cohesion- and confidence-building mirroring experiences. Later on in the therapy, he remarked offhandedly that there were times he wished he had "an inflatable Tom," referring to me, that he could bring out and consult at home or work. This led to an explicit discussion of his feelings about me—as "part father, part older brother, and part colleague."

INITIAL PHASE

Our initial sessions focused alternatingly on his depression and on his life story. He described his depression as being "like a screen or film between me and what I experience." He suspected both his parents had been depressed. He thought that perhaps his father had never gotten over his own brother's death by drowning—evidenced by the fact that he took his brother's name as his own for the rest of his life. His mother, he said, was never happy and also drank too much. Although she was very bright, she was also quite self-critical. And both of them, he felt, had never gotten over their firstborn son's dying just days after he had been born.

Mr. F. has an older sister, his parents' second child, who lives with her husband and two children in another state. She left home to attend college when he started elementary school. He felt that in many respects, he was raised as if an only child. He recalled often feeling "caught in the middle" between his "continually bickering" parents. He also remembered feeling that he could "never be good enough" to make up for the child who had died. He is married and he and his wife have a daughter.

Mr. F. had two prior experiences with psychotherapy that had been helpful in a number of ways–one of which was some relief from his depression. Some time after the conclusion of each of these therapeutic episodes, however, his depression had returned. This brought us to the possibility of seeking a consultation with a psychiatrist. He pursued this and was prescribed Zoloft, 75 mg. daily. He responded well to the medication which took effect in the time between our third and fourth sessions.

Even without the mind-clearing benefits of the medication, however, there were several opportunities for therapeutic interventions during the first three sessions. At the end of the first session, he asked for my reactions to his story. I said that as he knew from his own work, what he had just told me could be considered as one version or story of his life. Would he be interested, I asked, in using the therapy sessions, in part, to expand that story, or at least consider ways in which it might be expanded? He was interested and asked me for an example. I had noticed that when he spoke of his father, he seemed moved by feelings of disappointment and some shame. So I said that it struck me that most of his memories of his father were not very positive and that I found myself wondering whether there might not be more to the man and his life. Specifically, I asked Mr. F. if there were any positive ways in which he honored his father in his own life. He found the question intriguing and said he would give it some thought in preparation for his next session.

In that session he said that he realized that while there were some superficial ways in which he honored his father in a positive way (keeping some of his tools and wearing hats like his father had) most of his honoring was of a negative kind–such as staying emotionally withdrawn from his wife and daughter like his father had and drinking to escape more than he really thought he should. Thinking about the question had led him to realize that he was working mostly from negative memories of his father, so the prospect of using the therapy to expand that story by adding some positive memories appealed to him. He realized that there were large periods of his father's life about which he knew little, if anything.

In the third session, ten days after he had begun taking the Zoloft but before he had registered any beneficial effects from it, he arrived looking more depressed than previously and complaining that he had a very difficult week, "struggling, lethargic, resigned." After exploring and eliminating several possible reasons (something at home or work, our discussion in the previous session, disappointment that the Zoloft wasn't working more quickly), I asked if it could be an anniversary reaction of any kind. It was–the anniversary of his mother's death five years earlier. This led to a discussion of his plans to visit her gravesite and my suggestion that he pay attention to any unresolved feelings about his mother and their relationship that the visit might stir up.

In the following (fourth) session, Mr. F. said that while at his mother's gravesite, he realized that he felt she considered him a "special but fragile boy" during most of his boyhood years. In our discussion of the meanings and implications of that story, I asked him if he thought the fragile part had anything to do with his older brother's death while still an infant, suggesting that in some ways the "special but fragile" story might be more about his mother's reactions to the prior child's death than about him. Although we considered his talking with his sister about her memories of their parents, he took no action on this for some time.

The fifth session took on the significance of a "breakthrough" for him and also marked a shift in emphasis on my part from a narrative and multigenerational focus to one of self-psychologically informed responsiveness, listening in the empathic mode and speaking in the interpretive mode. Mr. F. began the session by jokingly saying that although the Zoloft was obviously helping, it was not the miracle drug he had been hoping for. He felt muddled at work. He had promised one of his administrative superiors a memorandum that he just could not bring himself to write– mainly, it turned out, because he knew that in effect he would be disagreeing with a position this administrator had taken. Then there was his own writing. He had published only one thing from his dissertation, completed nine years prior. He was generally self-critical in describing himself in all of this.

I responded first by exploring the details of the memorandum and his reluctance to tell the administrative superior something he might not want to hear. We discussed the tone and structure of the memorandum and some hypothetical phrases he might use, ultimately finding some words that he felt expressed his thoughts accurately. Part of this discussion involved exploring his anticipations as to his superior's responses to each of the hypothetical phrases. He felt that he was addressing a recurring difficulty in his life, as he put it, "equating getting love with being good." Contradicting his superior in the memorandum was being bad and that would result in his not being loved–or, in this context, not being liked. This "false equation" reinforced his tendency to inhibit himself in all of his relationships, he said, and this was something else he hoped to get out of the therapy: "a sense of his own agency and an integration of these different parts of myself."

Then we moved on to his own writing. I asked him to give me some idea of what work he had in progress and particularly what he felt most strongly about, what he wanted to write about first. He went into some detail about a paper that had been well received at a conference but that had not been accepted for publication by the journal to which he had submitted it. He also complained about how difficult it was to get the blocks of time he needed to write and we commiserated. Following 15-20 minutes of our brainstorming about how he could get started, he concluded the session by describing a general plan of action that he thought would be feasible and satisfying. He left the session saying how helpful the conversation had been and thanking me. I said he was welcome and that I wanted to read a copy of the article we had spent the most time discussing so that I could become more informed about his field and what he was working on.

Mr. F. arrived for the sixth session with a copy of his manuscript for me. He was visibly upbeat and described a newly found level of energy and productivity at work, making progress on several fronts: his own writing, his relationship with his administrative superior, and the successful negotiation of an academic appointment within his department that he had been hoping would come through for some months. He also noted that, in thinking about his therapy, some new themes were emerging for him, related to our discussion of his equating getting love with being good. He said that he had become aware of other false equations and dichotomies that were troubling him, such as kindness equaling weakness, that love and sex were incompatible, and that caring meant being involved emotionally with the other to the point of sacrificing his own needs and wants.

These two sessions illustrate several aspects of how a self-psychologically informed psychotherapy works. In the fifth session the therapist listens to the complaints of an enfeebled and immobilized self and responds by immersing himself in the details of the client's struggle for some self-sustaining direction and energy. The client responds by reconstructing his current difficulties as a recurring difficulty for himself that has a theme—equating getting love with being good. This clearer comprehension of self is an example of higher functioning made possible by the concurrent participation in a selfobject experience. The therapist allows himself to be used by the client in a particular psychological way that the client needs in order to gain coherence, direction, and energy. In this instance, it appears to be primarily a twinship selfobject experience with aspects of mirroring (acknowledging his frustrated ambitions) and idealizing (encouraging him to pursue his ideals).

The increased vitality, direction, and productivity so manifest in the sixth session suggest that the self-selfobject experience in the fifth session had some enduring effects both in his work life and in his own psychotherapeutic process. The false dichotomy idea resulted from his seeing himself in some greater depth and breadth–in part due to his participation in the therapist's process of getting to know him in that way.

By the sixth session, then, the value of combining narrative theory, self psychology, and a multigenerational family systems perspective on this case had become apparent. Mr. F.'s story about himself–encapsulated in his statement about having to be good to be loved–had emerged within a self-psychologically informed therapeutic dialogue. The origins of this story were located within his own multigenerational family context. The psychotherapeutic process itself was manifesting traditional signs that it was working; Mr. F. was understanding more about himself and bringing it up in the sessions, broadening and deepening the reflective process. In addition, he was functioning better in his work.

There is no question about the contribution of the Zoloft to these improvements; it made it easier for him participate in the psychotherapy and to make use of the therapy in his life. He no longer experienced the screen, or film, between himself and his experience.

The therapy continued to be shaped by these three theories over the remaining 24 sessions. Before proceeding to discuss them, however, it is important to be clear about what are the major intersecting ideas from these theories.

NARRATIVE THEORY

Narrative theory is an evolving set of ideas that flow from one main idea, namely, that each of us gives meaning to our selves and our experience in the world by organizing our understanding of ourselves and our experiences in the form of stories or narratives that we tell (or narrate) to both ourselves and others (Bruner, 1990, 1986). While there are many implications of this idea, the ones I wish to emphasize for this discussion follow:

1. that the desire to organize understanding via narrative seems to be an innate characteristic of humans;
2. that there appear to be two concurrent versions of any narrative–a personal or private version and a social or public version–that reciprocally shape each other;

3. that all narratives, both personal and social, are the products of conversations and therefore emergent or continually evolving;
4. that personal narratives have a strong, if not binding, influence on behavior; and
5. that successful revision of one's personal or private narrative depends on finding a conversant–in this context, a therapist–with whom one can reconstruct one's private, personal narrative through a public (i.e., two-person) conversation.

Several other authors already have begun applying narrative theory to the therapeutic process (Spence, 1982; Saari, 1991; White & Epston 1990; Epston and White 1992; Schafer, 1992; Ornstein, A., 1994; White, 1995) because, as Riessman (1994) puts it: "Clients typically represent experience in this [narrative] way to clinicians who help retell and reconstruct new, more fulfilling narratives" (p. 67). The issue I wish to pursue here is how the therapist participates in conversations with the client so as to promote a retelling and reconstruction that is indeed more fulfilling for the client. To put this in the form of a question: How does the clinician know what to say in the (public) conversation with the client that will enhance the private conversation the client continues to have with himself?

This question raises the related one of how to consider the multiple selves implied in many narratives. Schafer (1992) provides one of the best examples of this problem in asking: How many selves or types of selves are implied in the following account?

> I told my friend that whenever I catch myself exaggerating, I bombard myself with reproaches that I never tell the truth about myself, so that I end up feeling rotten inside, and even though I tell myself to cut it out, that there is more to me than that, that it is important for me to be truthful, I keep dumping on myself. (p. 25)

As Schafer himself points out, these multiple versions of self that occur in both everyday and therapeutic conversations can be distinguished according to whether they correspond to a functional or a representational self (p. 22). For us to consider how the therapist discerns and responds to the functional self with respect to the (storied) representational selves, it is necessary to set forth some ideas from self psychology.

SELF PSYCHOLOGY

Self psychology is a relatively recent development within psychoanalysis that is now recognized as a radical departure from Freud's world-view and theories of mental functioning, as well as a powerful alternative paradigm for understanding the therapeutic process (P. Ornstein, 1993). This theory is also an evolving set of ideas that flow from one main idea, namely, that the self, as "an independent center of perception and initiative" (Kohut, 1977: 93-100), requires certain kinds of responses from others for its own development, cohesion, vitality, productivity, and capacity to relate to others harmoniously (Kohut, 1984: 52).

These responses are of a particular kind. They are ones in which others communicate their understanding of us and what we want to achieve for ourselves in a way that energizes and inspires us to express ourselves and pursue our ideals by developing the mental and interpersonal skills to do so. Such responses also include, of course, the understanding that comforts and calms during reactive moments provoked by life's frustrations and disappointments.

What is most defining of these kinds of responses is that the self experiences the psychological function being provided by the other as though it comes from within, a psychological event or process that is both enlivening and structure-building. (This is why Kohut referred to them as "selfobject experiences"—without the hyphen—to signify the psychological nature of the interpersonal process.)

The structures that get built are the many (once ego, now self) psychological functions pertaining to monitoring, maintaining, and restoring self-esteem; self-regulation of emotions, cognitions, and behaviors; and interpersonal relatedness. Successful psychological development requires several collaborators over a lifetime (Galatzer-Levy & Cohler, 1993). And even successful functioning in the present, in real time, depends on access to these types of experiences.

As with narrative theory, there are also many implications that stem from this idea, including these that I wish to emphasize:

1. that the (functional) self is, in effect, constituted through a life-long series of interactions with others;
2. that the critical feature of these interactions is the experience of being understood in depth;
3. that being understood in depth is vitalizing for the self but that disappointments in being understood are inevitable;
4. that the ability to participate in the process of correcting misunderstandings is an acquired capacity; and
6. that learning to correct such misunderstandings depends on the empathic participation of an other.

Since self psychology has evolved in the context of clinical practice, the body of literature applying this theory to the therapeutic process is now quite extensive. Although most of this literature initially was published by psychoanalysts for other psychoanalysts, more recently clinical psychologists and social workers have begun to apply the theory to clinical work with a variety of problems and populations (Elson, 1986; Gardner, 1991; Jackson, 1991; Young, 1994). Most of this literature continues to struggle with the question posed above about how the clinician can best respond in therapeutic conversations with clients. Some progress on this question can be made now if we explore some of the connections between narrative theory and self psychology.

Both narrative theory and self psychology view the self as "dialogue dependent" (Bruner, 1990: 101). All of us are continually evolving as independent centers of perception and initiative through dialogues with others. What moves each of us along our unique developmental pathways is the recurring experience of revising our understanding of our selves and our experience in discourse with others. The impetus for these dialogues is that the self is continually encountering aspects of self and experience (disturbances in the field of self-experience) that are not adequately organized by the existing personal narrative. The self seeks repair of these ruptures in the structure of its personal narrative through a social process of telling that allows for a revision in the narrative. These are therapeutic conversations.

The success of these therapeutic conversations is determined by whether the conversants can negotiate a new understanding of the teller's disturbances that is vitalizing. That is, an understanding that makes it possible for the self to understand the disturbances in a (revised) way that enhances the continued pursuit of ambitions and aspirations. For Mr. F., this vitalizing process began with the realization that there was more to his story about himself as the "special but fragile" son of depressed and alcoholic parents who could only be loved if he was good—meaning compliant and obedient to the point of suppressing his natural assertiveness and initiative. That possibility was introduced by the therapist.

The quality of the therapist's participation in these conversations is central to their success (defined as promoting the client's continued pursuit of ambitions and aspirations). The significance of what is told must be understood in the context of the teller's personal narrative (or life) as constructed by the teller as well as in the context of the telling of it (the client's relationship with the therapist). Both understandings depend on the capacity of the therapist to achieve an empathic understanding of the teller's self in the narrative process, as well as in the story itself.

It is the therapist's challenge to hear those experiences recounted in the narrative that are the sources of disruptions in the client's subjective experience of coherence, vitality, productivity, and harmony and to question them in a manner that evokes the client's curiosity. When these questions and the conversations they induce generate more balanced narratives, they are typically accompanied by incremental advances in coherence, vitality, productivity, and harmony—within the client and with others.

Of course, if the client does not feel safe emotionally in the relationship with the therapist or if the therapist's questions are experienced by the client as judgmental, the process reverses and the client's self-state stalls or regresses. This is why the empathic listening posture of the therapist is so important; the client must feel understood before it is possible to consider alternative understandings. In a similar way, the tentative nature of the therapist's interpretative posture is also important, since the client's interpretations, ultimately, are what make change possible (Ornstein, P. & Ornstein, A., 1985).

A MULTIGENERATIONAL FAMILY SYSTEMS PERSPECTIVE

The addition of a multigenerational family systems perspective provides a way for the clinician and client to locate many of the origins of the client's personal narrative and a useful context for assessing their significance. In addition, the multigenerational family system is also a resource offering multiple opportunities for new information and alternative perspectives that can yield revisions of personal narratives into ones that are more fulfilling and, in a word, vitalizing for the client's self (Freeman, 1992).

Many of the stories presented by clients in therapeutic conversations are about troubles or disturbances in their experiences of themselves with members of their families of origin. Or, to put it another way, many of the complaints presented by clients about their relationships with themselves and with others can be viewed as residual versions of similar difficulties they have experienced within their families of origin (Bowen, 1976; Freeman, 1981). Frequently, these stories also contain information about how the client has been heard and understood (or not) historically.

Examining these stories for their implications in the present, locating their origins in time and place, and expanding or supplementing them with others' versions makes it possible for the client to revise and reconstruct these stories, which in turn leads to the cognitive, emotional, and behavioral repositioning of one's self as Freeman (1992b: 205) has described.

For clinicians, a multigenerational family systems perspective can provide a framework for guiding their participation in clients' attempts to negotiate revisions in their personal narratives. What follows is a continuation of the therapeutic process of Mr. F. in which the ideas from narrative theory and self psychology set forth above are applied using a multigenerational family systems perspective as a guiding framework. The case summary resumes during the initial phase.

CONTINUATION OF INITIAL PHASE

The next six sessions were devoted to a process of elaborating Mr. F.'s understanding of himself in his multigenerational context. He told of his life-long desire to have a secret life, a "sequestered self" we called it, and the enduring worry that he "had to watch who he was" lest his secret and more assertive self get out, be bad, and run the risk of losing love. While he was able to resolve this rather quickly in his work relationships, at home he still felt both stuck and false. Using the already established multigenerational context, we began to focus on Mr. F.'s relationships with his wife and daughter and how he felt his parents' relationships with each other and with him might be shaping his participation in interactions with his wife and daughter.

This culminated in the 10th session, when Mr. F. said that he could see how he was repeating a pattern of being good (but hating it and staying emotionally distant) with his wife and daughter that he had learned as a child from watching his father interact with him and his mother. Following this session, he succeeded in an attempt to resolve a disagreement with his wife without resorting to being good (going along with her) or withdrawing emotionally in resentment. Subsequently, he often referred to this conversation as a "watershed" session because it seemed to him to be the conversation that led to the experience of his being able to be both more integrated and assertive–that sense of "personal agency and integration" he had said he was seeking through psychotherapy.

This session reflected the combined value of using narrative theory, self psychology, and a multigenerational family systems perspective in therapeutic conversations. Mr. F. saw promise in the opportunity to change his story about himself. Gradually, a new understanding of himself began to emerge from our (public) conversations about aspects of himself that he (privately) found disturbing and embarrassing. His new understanding was made possible, in part, by the therapist's participation in the conversation, a participation that was both empathic and expansive. It was empathic, in self psychological terms, because the therapist was trying to get to know Mr. F. in psychological depth. It was expansive because the therapist's attempt to get to know Mr. F. in depth included understanding him and his life in his multigenerational context.

From the perspective of narrative theory, the process might be conceptualized as follows. The client's functional self (which I understand as Kohut's independent center of perception and initiative) begins therapy in a weakened state and produces various stories about his (representational) selves. These stories are typically of three types. One consists of stories about the self that wants to be, the yet unrealized, but true self. A second consists of stories about who, tragically, the client actually has become–stories of dysfunction and pain. A third consists of stories about how the client got this way–about how the self has suffered disabling tragedies, traumas, and insults.

If the client experiences the therapist as connected and understanding of the functional self in all its weakness and of how the various stories relate to the continuing struggle of the functioning self for vitality, then the client will permit the therapist to re-interpret and question these stories and will engage in the process as long as it is vitalizing for the functional self.

The impetus for the pursuit of revising his personal narrative came in part, of course, from Mr. F.'s dysphoria. But it also came from the therapist's understanding that many of Mr. F.'s prevailing stories were disabling ones, and from the therapist's curiosity about other versions. In the event, the nature of this discourse seemed to involve a combination of tentatively posed reconstructions by the therapist of Mr. F.'s stories that Mr. F. then reconstructed further and more accurately, and revisions initiated by Mr. F. in response to obtaining new information about himself and his family of origin.

MIDDLE PHASE

From this point on (13th through 22nd sessions), Mr. F.'s therapy seemed to develop a momentum of its own. He devoted a substantial amount of time–both within and outside of the sessions–to pursuing information about his father's and his father's brother's lives. This involved telephone and in-person conversations with his sister, a search of library files of local newspapers' obituaries, a review of cemetery records, and a visit to his father's family's gravesite. This last event was a surprisingly powerful experience. At the gravesite he saw, for the first time, a rose-marble gravestone with the names engraved on it: a great-grandmother on his father's side, his paternal grandparents, his paternal uncle who had died in the swimming accident, and his own infant brother who had actually been buried on top of his namesake paternal uncle.

For Mr. F., the significance of this was two-fold. First, he stated that he now felt less alone; seeing the gravestone left him feeling like he had family. Secondly, after seeing the gravestone he recalled being with his parents when they had picked it out. He remembered the event as a tortuous one because his parents were continually bickering over how many of the gravestone's surfaces should be polished; each additional surface added to the cost of it. He remembered feeling put in the middle and unable to state his own preference (polishing all sides). He dated the beginnings of his having to "lock away" his assertive self to this period of his life.

Then, the conversations with his sister led to his learning that she had saved some of their father's letters to her (after she had left home for college) in which he had written to her about her brother, Mr. F. Reading these letters, he said, showed him a different side of his father; a more caring, playful, and engaged man than the depressed, drinking, and emotionally remote father of his memory.

This thread of the therapy–interweaving the multigenerational perspective with the re-storying approach of narrative theory–culminated in the 20th session when he introduced a "shameful story" he had about himself and his father, dating to when Mr. F. was 16. The shameful story was that Mr. F.'s father, after three years of preparing Mr. F. to go hunting with him and his hunting buddy, did not invite him. Mr. F. believed, although he and his father had never discussed it, that this meant that his father thought that Mr. F. was a sissy.

Our discussion of "what else might have been going on" with Mr. F.'s father at the time, released a memory Mr. F. had forgotten. The memory was that Mr. F.'s father's hunting buddy had developed a heart condition that prohibited him from going hunting and that Mr. F.'s father had joined another small group of men for his annual fall hunting trip. Mr. F. recalled that his father really did not enjoy these men very much. They were coarse and rowdy and Mr. F.'s father soon stopped going hunting altogether. In Mr. F.'s reflection on this, it seemed to change the story from one in which his father considered him a sissy to one in which his father was protecting him from an unpleasant experience and an unwanted influence. We also discussed how the "shameful version" of this story reinforced the "special but fragile boy" story we had talked about previously and that both now could be viewed as only partially valid.

The therapy's momentum was evident in self psychological terms as well. Early on in this phase, he was disappointed and upset with me because I had discussed his adjustment to the Zoloft with his psychiatrist rather than directly with him. He felt that our relationship was a very important one to him and that my speaking to the psychiatrist rather than directly to him was a betrayal of his trust in me. Then, his continuing struggle to hold his own in his relationship with his wife had him wondering if I thought they should pursue couples therapy and, if so, would I provide it. This led directly to my asking him how he felt about me and he described me as alternatively "father figure, older brother, and colleague." We agreed that, at this time, our relationship was so important to him in a number of ways that it would not be a good idea for him if I were to become his and his wife's couples therapist. A few sessions later while confirming our schedule of appointments, he remarked that he had me "scheduled in forever."

Then he had a dream about therapy, specifically about having "difficulty getting to me" and having to "get through this large crowd in your waiting room." He thought it was a dream about ending the therapy—"how, when, why?"—and we had another discussion about the ways in which his relationship with me was helpful to him. He felt that, while he continued to benefit from the (fatherly, brotherly, collegial) help I provided, he had gotten what he had sought therapy for initially and he was wondering how we would end. My response was to agree that the dream was about ending but also about "getting through all the therapy" in order to "finish the job" and end with a sense of completion. Since he wanted to end by a certain date for both family and financial reasons, I suggested that he think about increasing the frequency of his sessions to once weekly at a reduced fee and setting a specific date for ending. If the suggestion appealed to him, we would negotiate a revised fee beginning with his making an offer based on what he thought he could afford.

Mr. F.'s reaction to this offer had the unintended effect of revealing to himself that, to his surprise, he felt some resistance, both to ending and to finishing the job. He was struck by how the offer was asking him to be both honest and assertive with me—that is, to say what *he* wanted and to resolve the "good/bad split in my identity" by asserting what he wanted directly, rather than to appear to be good but to try to get what he really wanted in some indirect way. All of our reflective conversation about these issues seemed very important to him and in the end, he decided to come weekly, and asked for a fifty percent reduction in the fee, which I accepted.

ENDING PHASE

The initial effect of the new arrangement on the therapy was a return to his preoccupation with himself in his relationship with his wife. He talked about how he remembered his father obtaining private time and space within his relationship with Mr. F.'s mother and how he repeated his father's pattern of retreating emotionally in his relationship with his wife whenever she wanted more togetherness. Mr. F. thought that his guiding story was that "if you get close, you have to please"; if you want to pursue your own needs and wants, you have to "sneak it privately."

In our conversations about this it became clear that what Mr. F. was seeking was "a clear experience of himself" in his relationships. He did not want to continue to feel, as he did in most all of his relationships, that he "had to be good"–placate, please, or accommodate the other person in the hope of indirectly getting what he wanted, rather than asserting it directly.

Mr. F. focused mostly on his relationship with his wife–talking about how he could communicate more directly with her about his own needs, wants, and points of view, followed by a negotiation of their differences, rather than placating and then resenting her. All of this he discussed, without prompting, in the context of what he recalled observing and experiencing with his parents.

As the ending date approached, Mr. F. devoted more time in each session to the topic of ending and reviewing what he had achieved through the therapy. He acknowledged that even though he was not "completely finished (Is one ever?)," he felt "cognitively and affectively ready." He said that he was very pleased with the progress he had made with himself, his work, and his relationships with his wife and daughter–even though he continued to feel vulnerable in his relationship with his wife. We agreed that at some future time they would do well to pursue couples therapy. His concluding reflections on himself were that he "had never felt this comfortable" with himself and his life. A follow-up telephone call four months after the last session verified that Mr. F. continued to feel that way and that he was doing well both at work and at home.

CONCLUSION

As Mr. F. would be quick to point out, this paper itself is but one version of the story of his therapy. As every therapist and client knows, psychotherapy is a much more complex and multi-layered process than any written summary can hope to capture.

This version was written to illustrate how the ideas of narrative theory and self psychology can be applied productively within a multigenerational family systems perspective. The story Mr. F. had evolved about himself prior to beginning therapy was very much influenced by his experiences within his family of origin which, in turn, very much influenced his behavior in his family of procreation and in his work.

Telling a (public) version of his personal (private) narrative to a therapist whose participation was informed by self psychology, narrative theory, and a multigenerational perspective allowed Mr. F. to examine and reconstruct some of his more powerful personal narratives in ways that were more vitalizing, providing him with the sense of personal agency and integration he was seeking. These revisions then made it possible for him to take a new, more engaged, and fulfilling position with himself, his deceased parents, his sister, his wife and daughter, and his work.

REFERENCES

Bowen, M. (1976). *Family therapy in clinical practice*. New York: Jason Aronson.

Bruner, J. (1986). *Actual minds, possible worlds*. Cambridge, MA: Harvard University Press.

Bruner, J. (1990). *Acts of meaning*. Cambridge, MA: Harvard University Press.

Elson, M. (1986). *Self psychology in clinical social work*. New York: W. W. Norton.

Epston, D. & White, M. (1992). *Experience, contradiction, narrative and imagination: Selected papers of David Epston and Michael White, 1989-1991*. Adelaide, South Australia: Dulwich Centre Publications.

Freeman, D. (1981). *Techniques of family therapy*. New York: Jason Aronson.

Freeman, D. (1992a). *Multigenerational family therapy*. New York: The Haworth Press, Inc.

Freeman, D. (1992b). *Family therapy with couples: The family-of-origin approach*. Northvale, New Jersey: Jason Aronson.

Galatzer-Levy, R. & Cohler, B. (1993). *The essential other: A developmental psychology of the self*. New York: Basic Books.

Gardner, J. (1991). The application of self psychology to brief psychotherapy, *Psychoanalytic Psychology, 8*: 477-500.

Gergen, K. (1991). *The saturated self*. New York: Basic Books.

Horner, E. (1995). The meeting of two narratives. *Clinical Social Work Journal, 23*, 1: 9-19.

Jackson, H., ed. (1991). *Using self psychology in psychotherapy*. Northvale, NJ: Jason Aronson.

Kohut, H. (1971). *The analysis of the self*. New York: International Universities Press.

Kohut, H. (1977). *The restoration of the self*. New York: International Universities Press.

Kohut, H. (1978). *The search for the self*, 4 vols., P. Ornstein, (ed.) Madison, Connecticut: International Universities Press.

Kohut, H. (1984). *How does analysis cure?* Chicago: The University of Chicago Press.

Kohut, H. & Wolf, E. (1978). The disorders of the self and their treatment: An outline, *International Journal of Psychoanalysis, 59*: 413-25.

Ornstein, A. (1994). Trauma, memory, and psychic continuity. In A. Goldberg (Ed.), *A decade of progress: Progress in self psychology, Volume 10*. Hillsdale, N. J.: The Analytic Press.

Ornstein, P. (1993). The clinical impact of the psychotherapist's view of human nature, *The Journal of Psychotherapy Practice and Research, 2*: 193-204.

Ornstein, P. & Ornstein, A. (1985). Clinical understanding and explaining: The empathic vantage point. In A. Goldberg, ed., *Progress in Self Psychology*, Vol. 1: 43-61. New York: Guilford.

Ornstein, A. & Ornstein, P. (1990). The process of psychoanalytic psychotherapy: A self-psychological perspective. In *Annual Review of Psychiatry, 9*: 323-340. Washington, DC: American Psychiatric Press.

Palombo, J. (1985). Depletion states and selfobject disorders, *Clinical Social Work Journal, 13*,1: 32-49.

Pardeck, J., Murphy, J., & Choi, J. (1994). Some implications of postmodernism for social work practice, *Social Work, 39*, 4: 343-6.

Riessman, C. (1994). Narrative approaches to trauma. In C. Riessman (Ed.), *Qualitative studies in social work research* (pp. 67-71). Thousand Oaks, CA: Sage Publications, Inc.

Saari, C. (1991). *The creation of meaning in clinical social work*. New York: The Guilford Press.

Schafer, R. (1992). *Retelling a life: Narration and dialogue in psychoanalysis*. New York: Basic Books.

Spence, D. (1982). *Narrative truth and historical truth: Meaning and interpretation in psychoanalysis*. New York: W. W. Norton.

White, M. (1995). *Re-Authoring Lives: Interviews and Essays*. Adelaide South Australia: Dulwich Centre Publications.

White, M. & Epston, D. (1990). *Narrative means to therapeutic ends*. New York: W. W. Norton & Co.

White, M. & Epston, D. (1992). *Experience, Contradiction, Narrative and Imagination*. Adelaide South Australia: Dulwich Centre Publications.

Young, T. (1994). Environmental modification in clinical social work: A self-psychological perspective. *Social Service Review, 68*, 202-18.

Chapter 8

Saturday's Children:
A Discussion
of George Steiner's *Real Presences*

Barbara J. Socor

REAL PRESENCES, Steiner, George, ed. *Chicago, Illinois: University of Chicago Press, 1991, 236 pages (paperback), $12.95.*

In a postmodern age, the significance of psychoanalysis may rest in it's capacity to signify nothing. Perhaps one of the more unsettling intellectual developments of recent decades has been the sustained theoretical assault upon the idea of meaning as it has been given particular voice by deconstructive theory and its adherents in the field of literary criticism. Meaning, as a fundamental construct suggesting an actual and discoverable significance that inheres in actions, in lives, in the very cosmos, is dismantled. Meaning is reduced to its component verbal elements and found to say nothing. It has been deconstructed, reduced to a series of words which have lost their fixed relationship to actual things in the actual world. Authors are merely starting points in their own texts, their affirmed narrative intentions subject to other confirmed readings. Deconstructive theory, as it asserts the endless malleability of textual intent, and the postmodern ethic, as it is disinclined to assign any meaning to meaning, have recalled the long-standing cultural concession to transcendence. And just as legitimate textual references have been subject to postmodern rewrites–in a

Barbara J. Socor, PhD, MSW, CSW, is a faculty member of Iona College, Department of Social Work.

[Haworth co-indexing entry note]: "Saturday's Children: A Discussion of George Steiner's *Real Presences*" Socor, Barbara J. Co-published simultaneously in *Journal of Analytic Social Work* (The Haworth Press, Inc.) Vol. 3, No. 2/3, 1996, pp. 157-166; and: *Narration and Therapeutic Action: The Construction of Meaning in Psychoanalytic Social Work* (ed: Jerrold R. Brandell) The Haworth Press, Inc., 1996, pp. 157-166. Single or multiple copies of this article are available from The Haworth Document Delivery Service [1-800-342-9678, 9:00 a.m. - 5:00 p.m. (EST) E-mail address: get info@haworth.com].

sense to erasure–so too has the individual self, once undisputed author of its own storied life, come to the editing table in search of itself.

Thus freed from presumptions of fixed and antecedent meaning, all referents–and perhaps especially self-references–become suspect. Deconstructive theory effectively condemns significance, expelling it from the house of language to become a nomad among perpetually shifting signifiers. Now, words simply signal other words, and everything is potentially significant–and finally meaningless. Absent a fixed referent toward which all things tend, what is there? Without an overarching source of truth, who am I? And what enduring determinations can psychoanalysis make about the self that the self, in its postmodern indeterminacy, cannot redact?

These are some of the central questions implied by George Steiner in his brilliant set of essays, *Real Presences*. Conceived as pieces in literary criticism, they may perhaps be best described as philosophical ponderings on the nature of language and the aesthetic enterprise in the absence of metaphysical meaning. Taken in the aggregate, these essays examine the ontological postulate of transcendence as it has long been associated with the human impulse toward creative activity, exploring the view that an antecedent faith in some metaphysical actuality inhabiting a seemingly indifferent universe–a *real presence* in an apparent absence–remains the dynamic behind all such activity. They further weigh how creativity and language can remain viable in the wake of a (theoretical) deconstruction of meaning. Singly, each essay engages a discrete aspect of this central question: What is the role of creativity in the aftermath of transcendence?

In the first, "A Secondary City," Steiner undertakes to explore and illuminate the assertion that all efforts to communicate meaning through language contain a necessary assumption of presence, particularly and especially the presence of a theologically immersed transcendence. In the second, "The Broken Contract," he pursues what is conceived to be the now dissolved but hitherto long-standing collective assumption of congruence between the word and the object it speaks. In the third essay, "Presences," Steiner develops his contention that "there is language . . . because there is 'the other.'" All are variations on the theme of transcendence, its role in creativity, and the meaning of the aesthetic in the wake of its passing.

Thus, the central assertion of "A Secondary City" is that the act of speaking is an act of faith, testimony to a belief in the presence and receptivity of an other, and ultimately of "The Other." We venture to create, Steiner says, to make sound and to fashion signs, on the *"wager"* that someone is listening and ready to respond. This wager, this distinctly human gamble on recognition, informs the religious impulse, the aesthetic urge, and, I would add, is the dynamic behind our psychoemotional lives as they are daily lived.

Steiner contends that the very impulse to create, to construct a meaningful meaning from the fact of being, is born of a prior belief in an actual receptivity in the world, which is nothing less than a wager on transcendence. We do not speak on the belief that no one is listening. On the contrary, words are hurled into the darkness, and upon the "face of the deep," in the (unspoken) conviction that some other is present in the absence. Thus does Steiner conceive of artistic creation as an invitation to dialogue; speech as an invocation, and language a prayer.

Steiner's wager on the receptive presence of the other is, of course, not restricted to the realm of the aesthetic. Clearly, the client crossing the threshold of a consulting room gambles on being heard and recognized. Every client brings, along with all sorrow and all regret, along with all longing and all fear, some antecedent, and overarching–i.e., *transcendent*– confidence (or hope) in the receptive presence of the unknown other counselor, consultant, or analyst. Therapeutic engagement too is an act of faith. The desire for the recognition and associated affirmation of an other surpasses sorrow and regret, reaches beyond longing and fear, which by themselves, absent any conviction in something "more," and "else," could not propel the individual through the door. It is, I believe, this very faith that one may be heard, and has a chance of being understood, that is the dynamic driving the analytic hour. Where there is no such belief in one's ultimate confirmation, there we encounter abysmal despair. But where there is a willingness toward speech, toward any voluntary act in which I declare myself, there also do I declare my readiness to speculate, indeed to bet, that you are listening, or looking (or reading). It is a bet that there is something rather than nothing, and it is this wager, says Steiner, that propels the creative impulse. A profoundly optimistic view, it rejects an indifferent universe. Significance is born of, and borne upon, the expectation of reception. It cannot fall on deaf ears or pass before blind eyes. It is generated in the assumption of hospitality.

Knowledge of the other, Steiner avows, rests in *immediacy*. It is a distinctly "primary" transaction in which the reader and the text admit of no intermediary voice. Potential meaning, riding on the wager that there is an audience, becomes actual meaning as the listener (the other) responds to and thus knows the declarer (the other) through a direct encounter with a creative declaration of presence that is the work of art. Indeed, to *immediately* experience someone else's work is to feel a sense of inarticulate familiarity with a musical passage or a landscape view. It is quite literally to be touched by, to know the real presence of, "otherness." We are reminded here of the important and elegant work of the British psychoanalyst Christopher Bollas, particularly as he has conceived of the *transformational object* to signify those experiences which occur prior to language and so are thus bound to be rediscovered only in an untranslatable immanence. Meaning is primarily an unmediated event, and attempts at interpretation are, Steiner suggests, secondary.

Thus, the realization of meaning is often a preinterpretive *adventure* whose occurrence provides the occasion for "commentary without end." For, as Steiner himself comments, "the primary text," or, from a clinical perspective, the precipitating event, "is only the remote font of autonomous exegetic proliferation" (p. 39). That is, the initially mysterious and often inexplicable creative moment of meaning–of being–becomes a distant starting point for an endless deciphering not unrelated, as Steiner observes, to myriad Talmudic commentaries upon an originally unsayable and transcendent encounter with profound otherness.

So Steiner's "secondary city" is inhabited by interpreters. Here, residents labor to make primary transactions available to secondary reflection by engaging in a deliberate effort to recollect assorted and selected pieces of "immediacy," making them (theoretically) intelligible as they are placed within some explanatory frame. By conducting via translation the enigma of an other's being, interpreters engage in an authentic effort to extend what we dimly apprehend of the other by speaking of it again–by recalling it and seeking to hold it before the mind's eye. So the literary critic, in a genuine response to a work, undertakes to answer the declaration of presence which that work bespeaks. So, too, the counselor and the analyst.

Perhaps it may be said that the essence of therapeutic action, as well as its enactment by therapist and client, resides in the creation of a narrative tale, a kind of personal *Ur-text*, wherein mute apprehension is rendered articulate comprehension through the interpretive alchemy of language. And the tale thus jointly constructed becomes the bridge upon which analyst and client may meet, and where the self may encounter its particular meaning as it confronts the real presence of the other.

But there is a dilemma inherent in commentary. For, Steiner says, it is in its very nature an unending exercise, upon which closure is often summarily and even capriciously imposed. There is always something more to be said, running the risk that the act of interpretation (aesthetic or psychological) becomes an end in itself, its intended explanatory purpose sacrificed as the hermeneutic enterprise becomes its own justification. Equally hazardous, interpretation may, in the interests of declaring certainty and constraining anxiety, existential or otherwise, be arbitrarily halted.

Thus the "responsible answerability" of meaningful interpretation must negotiate the Scylla of unending commentary and the Charybdis of premature closure. Whereas the former threatens a kind of "banishment" from the precipitant source of commentary, the latter imperils creativity. Steiner claims that in the first circumstance, whether addressing a work of art or an act of psychic assertion, "there is a sense in which all commentary is itself an act of exile" (p. 40) which keeps one forever apart from the object (of desire). Premature closure, however, by imposing a doctrinaire finality, endangers a rich and diversified knowledge of the source from which all subsequent interpretation springs. Speech is a wager on being heard, but endless speech serves only to deafen one to the other. Yet foreshortened speech itself forecloses the prospect of infinite encounter.

The dilemma posed by interpretation is not lost on the analytic project, particularly in its methodology of free association. How and where one begins, and when and where one determines an end is a function of *a priori* theoretical assumptions or contingent events. Thus does Steiner observe that "the analyst's decision to interrupt the unwinding progression, to punctuate what is, in the most direct sense, an unending phrase, at the close, say, of sixty minutes or before the summer break, is arbitrary" (p. 45). In introducing this quality of ceaseless signification–of meaning without end–psychoanalysis is challenged to contemplate how its own theoretical determinism may accommodate a postmodern indeterminacy.

The second essay, "The Broken Contract," tracks this idea of indeterminacy to the very character of speech. Whereas every other human capability encounters an upper limit beyond which it cannot go, language knows no boundary. It is possible to say *anything*, for the inventions available to language are limitless. All things said may be unsaid; all directions taken, reversed; all time lost, found; for "language," Steiner avows, "need halt at no frontier, not even . . . death" (p. 54). Speech may utter the infinite, for the boundless, intrinsically anarchic nature of words admits all manner of being, all innovations of identity.

Thus, in the same sense that language is, in Steiner's phrase, "possessed by the dynamics of fiction," are the truths of our lives driven by invention; the "true" self secured in story. We can, perhaps must, conceive ourselves, for language–an inherently fictive tool–is what is available for "truth making," and the only meaningful truth we speak is the one we contrive to say. And because we can unsay it we can alter the truth of our lives, and say new true lives; we can become other than we are and not who we said we were. And we can claim no greater reality for one tale than for another, save that we choose to believe this version, to privilege it over an other.

Now, perhaps since Spence, we have increasingly taken into account—and into the consulting room—the variations on truthful experiences presented by history and by narrative. What Steiner offers, in his contemplation of the boundless character of language, is another way to consider the shadow that the facticity of death casts upon the couch. Indeed, Steiner's writings can be seen to make of the indeterminant character of speech a metaphoric preparation for one's determined end.

It is a vital paradox of being that the limitless character of our most human capacity contains within its own structure its own delimitation. For we recognize that every narrative has a beginning, a middle, and an end. No good story overstays its welcome and "once upon a time" is always followed by "the end." Indeed, we regularly depict our lives in this orderly fashion, though we know they are not experienced thus. In fact, it may be an imperative residing within the configurations of both language and mind which compels closure. Steiner's assertion that "in their terminal structure, narrations are rehearsals for death" (p. 141), underscores this contention. At the heart of all unpunctuated speech lies the period. All sentences are death sentences. Speech, however, does allow a metaphoric deferral by forestalling final punctuation. We continue to talk, as Scheherazade, for a thousand and one nights, charming fate, weaving immortality, talking to and in the face of death.

This essay abounds in questions which may be taken to the heart of psychoanalytic inquiry. Can we, for example, in light of the interminable play of words, and the determined end of life, posit a "linguistic death instinct," drawn by a narrative imperative to mirror in words the closure that will inevitably be played in life? Can the ceaseless run-on sentence that is the stream of unconsciousness be aiming to talk death to death?

Implied in all that we have addressed is the assumption that we are able to proclaim our existence because we rest in the assurance that there is a correlation—indeed a contract—between the word spoken and the thing it speaks, an actuality which inheres between word and world. This existential covenant between the speaker and a posited listener, a transcendent author, stipulates that in the seeming absence there resides a real presence whose "thereness" confers meaning "here."

This contract, Steiner indicates, was broken in the late nineteenth century and is associated, interestingly enough, with the literary dissolution of the "I" in the work of such (other) authors as Rimbaud and Mallarme. It is observed of these works that one of their essential feats was to deny the "I" sovereignty in its own psychic house. Self no longer addressed an accomplished unity—indeed, it has been deconstructed into many, and momentary selves each possessed of its own transitory truth. Along with

Saussure, whose upending contribution to modern thought consisted in the undoing of the sacred tie between word and world, these developments led to Steiner's time "after-Word."

This is a (postmodern) time in which the authority of the singular and central "I," of the long-standing *cogito* after all, falls, along with what Steiner has called the "covenant of reference." Without any actual and inherent referability of what we say to any overarching source "all bets are off," the wager on "real presence" is withdrawn and a "real absence" (of final meaning, ultimate authority, original sin or anything else) empties the world (of the Word).

The aesthetic concern for Steiner is how, and *if,* the encounter with music, with literature, with painting, "can be made intelligible, can be made answerable to the existential facts" (p. 134), in the real absence of any assumption of transcendence. What can art mean if there is no faith that it will be seen, or heard? This question too is not unrelated to the psychoanalytic endeavor as it asks what the self can mean without an other.

Decidedly one of Freud's more revolutionary contributions was the decentering of the psyche at the hands of the unconscious. For once an unconscious is proposed, particularly as it is buffeted by illogical, amoral, and temporally indifferent libidinal forces, the singular ego becomes "a poor creature" indeed, in service to many masters. The unconscious split the self and initiated its existential splintering. The self was no longer fully knowable to itself, and its meaning now lay beyond its own grasp. Long before deconstructive theory carried language to the abyss of meaning, Freud, among others, glimpsed into the very heart of psychic darkness. Perhaps with Steiner, we may wonder how psychoanalysis can refer to the client in the absence of any contract with meaning. And perhaps with Freud, and also with Lacan, we may ponder the significance of an unconscious wherein the endless combinations of meaning may offer the possibility of creating other endlessly spontaneous selves.

In this connection we reflect upon Steiner's observation that the "Freudian paradigm of the articulate psyche is poetic, is potentially self– and world–creating" (p. 108) precisely because it too subverts the (sensible) contract between word and world. Words, as they are unconsciously spoken, bear neither a logical nor a necessary relation to that of which they speak. For the unconscious, we know, is where "yes" may mean "no," and intensely professed love may signify unspeakable hate. Reaction formations and passive aggressions are the linguistic paradoxes regularly employed to point toward what may be finally unsayable and multiple truths. The libidinal unconscious is also polysemically perverse. Even as it relies upon language, psychoanalysis too has placed intentionality under siege.

Steiner's challenge, it seems to me, rests in determining how we may approach the question of meaning, and by extension, the meaning of being a cohesive and deliberately contrived self, in a world abandoned by the real presence of the other. If "all bets are off," and if we no longer posit a progenitor and sovereign arbiter, then we have become existentially fatherless. As Steiner puts it, "we stand orphaned," absent any transcendent inheritance, any parental guidance. How can we determine what the intent of anything may be, or if there is intent, if the proposition of real absence is controlling? For if "God the Father of meaning, in His authorial guise, is gone from the game: [then] there is no longer any privileged judge, interpreter or explicator who can determine and communicate the truth, the true intent of the matter" (p. 127). We're on our own.

Indeed, we have (theoretically) slain the Father, as Freud (that other theoretical Father, theoretically) knew we would. But in exchange we have won a radical freedom; tongue-tied no longer, we speak only to, and into, the silence, as unbounded in our being as limitless language permits us to say. In the presence of Steiner's "real absence" we speak in no expectation of response, nor hope of answer. We speak into the wind and engage our echo. And we inquire, in the wake of deconstructed metaphysical expectation, after the therapeutic status of the still-listening analyst. Is this other still (theoretically) a guide through the unknown psyche, or a co-conspirator in the construction of that psyche? Can we continue to bring to the analytic endeavor what we expect to find, or learn to find what we seek to bring to mind?

In the third essay of this collection, "Presences," the problem of the status of "the other," and the existential estrangement of the human condition is engaged a final time. The discussion opens with the assertion that we always "address ourselves in constant soliloquy," which is to say, of course, that we are here still wagering on a "real presence." Conversations with the self always address some postulated other, because language, and the mind itself, cannot sustain a monologue. It is this same premise of transcendent presence, which we have seen inform Steiner's other two essays, which here conjures soliloquy. This supposition also inheres in some of the more prominent of analytic explanatory systems.

Thus does psychoanalytic object relations theory stand upon the same postulate of presence. Emotional stability and psychic viability are, after all, couched within the receptive images of significant "others." There is no identity, and no ability to become an independently functioning self, if one has not internalized some analog of the actual, and psychologically transcendent other, making it authentically present to the psyche. Psychological object relations is fundamentally about successfully effecting this transformation of otherness into the presence of the self, indeed, one may say that the self *is* insofar as it is a collection of others. Internalization allows the successful self to construct a "portable presence" which authorizes an ongoing relationship to–soliloquy with–the other.

Steiner here ponders anew what artistic creation can be in a post-transcendent world, where the knowledge of presence–paradoxically experienced as an "absent 'thereness'"–is forgotten. And we add, what can psychological identity mean, what can the "I" meaningfully say of it's self, if the other is no longer spoken? In a world devoid of any real presence, am I also absent? Reversing Nietzsche, we may ask "If there is no other, how can I be?"

Steiner concludes his final essay in the collection by constructing an elegant metaphor designed to address this ontological conundrum of a world in which the idea of verticality–that is, of higher and deeper truths– is abandoned, and we have long since awoke from dreams of transcendence. He suggests that we stand between a prearticulate muteness and a postarticulate immanence, no longer blinking dumbly at dark canopies, not yet silently comprehending all vastness, we abide an endless while in the house of language, and pass our days patiently pondering our own questions, awaiting some other answers.

Steiner conceives of this time between silences as an eternally Sabbatarian anteroom, in which we wait upon the coming day. Familiar with the agonies, the estrangement, and the inevitability of death that is Friday, we strain toward affirmation, and the silent substantiation of life that is Sunday. Suspended between dumbly witnessing our death-delimited, singular existence and silently realizing its resurrection in some anticipated Utopia, we can only spend our Saturdays in waiting. In this construction, all hope, all imagining, and all speech, are Sabbatarian in character. They arise from the imposed necessity to *wait* for a response, during which endless existential time there will be, as T.S. Eliot reminds, "time yet for a hundred indecisions, and for a hundred visions and revisions," all of which constitute the infinity of aesthetic (and psychic) expression that the human mind is heir to.

Saturday's children, we labor on in the gardens of *Logos*, sowing neologisms, dining on word salad; inhabiting the past and speaking the future, we dream of waking. It is in this metaphoric sense that all analytic hours also convene on Saturday, and all client speakers seek to engage all therapeutic listeners in the vast waiting room that is always the psychological sixth day.

Such a vision invites reconceptualization, asking that we rethink the psychoanalytic hour and where we aim to be at its close. If we consider that upon entering the waiting room the client has already known some of the agonies, betrayals, and losses that are Friday's fare and if we consider that this client is willing to wager on the analytic response that may carry affirmation, self-realization, and the renewal that is Sunday's promise, we may well ask if it is the analytic task to assist in the realization of fulfillment, to achieve the epiphany of presence reserved for Sunday. Or in developing the craft of meaningful waiting, do we join with Scheherazade in deferring the close of day with one more of Saturday's beguiling tales? If there is a significant role for the psychoanalyst after Steiner's contract with correspondence has been abrogated, is it to seek its renovation or the spontaneity of which its dissolution speaks?

These beautifully crafted and deeply intelligent essays, in all their rich complexity, offer the analytic worker a variety of fertile and stimulating ways of approaching the challenges presented to our profession by deconstructive theory. For where the Author has been exiled, so too have all authors, and where there is no metaauthoritative reference, in text or word, to which we may refer our case, there is also no single personal story to invest with antecedent authenticity. Just as literary theory seeks to preserve the text without an author, so too may psychoanalysis aim to revaluate the self in the absence of the other. In closing, we invoke what may be characterized as Steiner's "wake-up call" for its potential to rouse analysis from a determinist sleep to meet Saturday's indeterminant challenge, thus: "We have far too long dreamt the lazy dreams of firm foundations, of theological-metaphysical guarantors and arbiters. The distant fathers (who never were) have left us" (p. 124). And in the time after the departure, we are free to create in the vast and open (ended) fields of mind and memory what we will.

REFERENCES

Bollas, C. (1987), *The Shadow of the Object*. New York: Columbia University Press.

Freud, S. (1915), The unconscious. *Standard Edition*, 14:161-204. London: Hogarth Press, 1957.

Freud, S. (1923), The ego and the id. *Standard Edition*, 19:1-59. London: Hogarth Press, 1961.

Lacan, J. (1953), The function and field of speech and language in psychoanalysis. In: *Ecrits. A Selection*, tr. A. Sheridan. New York: W.W. Norton, 1977, pp. 30-113.

Saussure, F. de (1915), *Course in General Linguistics*, tr. W. Baskin, ed. C. Bally & A. Sechehaye with A. Reidlinger. New York: Philosophical Library, 1959.

Spence, D. (1982), *Narrative Truth and Historical Truth*. New York: W.W. Norton.

Author Index

Subject Index

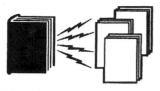

Haworth
DOCUMENT DELIVERY
SERVICE

This valuable service provides a single-article order form for any article from a Haworth journal.

- *Time Saving:* No running around from library to library to find a specific article.
- *Cost Effective:* All costs are kept down to a minimum.
- *Fast Delivery:* Choose from several options, including same-day FAX.
- *No Copyright Hassles:* You will be supplied by the original publisher.
- *Easy Payment:* Choose from several easy payment methods.

Open Accounts Welcome for ...
- Library Interlibrary Loan Departments
- Library Network/Consortia Wishing to Provide Single-Article Services
- Indexing/Abstracting Services with Single Article Provision Services
- Document Provision Brokers and Freelance Information Service Providers

---

MAIL or *FAX* THIS ENTIRE ORDER FORM TO:

Haworth Document Delivery Service
The Haworth Press, Inc.
10 Alice Street
Binghamton, NY 13904-1580

or FAX: 1-800-895-0582
or CALL: 1-800-342-9678
9am-5pm EST

PLEASE SEND ME PHOTOCOPIES OF THE FOLLOWING SINGLE ARTICLES:
1) Journal Title: _____
   Vol/Issue/Year: _____ Starting & Ending Pages: _____
   Article Title: _____

2) Journal Title: _____
   Vol/Issue/Year: _____ Starting & Ending Pages: _____
   Article Title: _____

3) Journal Title: _____
   Vol/Issue/Year: _____ Starting & Ending Pages: _____
   Article Title: _____

4) Journal Title: _____
   Vol/Issue/Year: _____ Starting & Ending Pages: _____
   Article Title: _____

(See other side for Costs and Payment Information)

COSTS: Please figure your cost to order quality copies of an article.

1. Set-up charge per article: $8.00
   ($8.00 × number of separate articles)   _____

2. Photocopying charge for each article:

   1-10 pages: $1.00   _____

   11-19 pages: $3.00   _____

   20-29 pages: $5.00   _____

   30+ pages: $2.00/10 pages   _____

3. Flexicover (optional): $2.00/article   _____

4. Postage & Handling: US: $1.00 for the first article/
   $.50 each additional article   _____

   Federal Express: $25.00   _____

   Outside US: $2.00 for first article/
   $.50 each additional article_____

5. Same-day FAX service: $.35 per page   _____

                    GRAND TOTAL: _____

METHOD OF PAYMENT: (please check one)

❑ Check enclosed   ❑ Please ship and bill. PO # _____
(sorry we can ship and bill to bookstores only! All others must pre-pay)

❑ Charge to my credit card: ❑ Visa; ❑ MasterCard; ❑ Discover;
❑ American Express;

Account Number:_____ Expiration date:_____

Signature: ✗_____

Name: _____ Institution: _____

Address: _____

_____

City: _____ State:_____ Zip:_____

Phone Number: _____ FAX Number: _____

MAIL or *FAX* THIS ENTIRE ORDER FORM TO:

Haworth Document Delivery Service | **or FAX**: 1-800-895-0582
The Haworth Press, Inc. | **or CALL**: 1-800-342-9678
10 Alice Street | 9am-5pm EST)
Binghamton, NY 13904-1580